P9-DEW-774

NO LONGER PROPERTY OF
FULLERTON PUBLIC LIBRARY

J
793.8
HED

USBORNE BOOK OF MAGIC TRICKS

Rebecca Heddle and Ian Keable

Edited by Christopher Rawson

Designed by Susie McCaffrey

CONTENTS

**Illustrated by Paul Sullivan, Kim Blundell
and Ian Thompson
Front cover illustrated by Martin Newton**

Magic is as much fun to perform as it is to watch. You don't need a big audience: these tricks work best in a small group. The next four pages give you hints on getting started and explain some useful skills and expressions.

How to learn tricks

First choose one trick you would like to learn, and try it out as you read the instructions. The pictures usually show the trick from your point of view. Then practise the trick without the book. Once you have conquered one trick, start on another.

Where to practise

Start by practising your tricks on your own. Make sure you practise in front of a mirror to see what your audience will see when you do each trick. As you gain confidence, try showing them to your friends, and ask them to criticize your performance.

Where to find props

You can make props for some tricks, and others are cheap to buy. You may need to borrow the rest, so make sure you ask first and always be very careful with borrowed props.

How to find something to wear

You can dress how you like to do magic. A good way of getting clothes quite cheaply is going to junk shops and flea-markets. You may find some unusual bargains.

Who to perform for

Almost everybody likes magic tricks, so there is no limit to the people you can perform for. Start with your family and friends, but try to pick a time when they will want to see some tricks.

What to say

What you say while performing is called your patter. It is a way you can add a personal touch to your magic. You can tell your audience about the history of the tricks or invent stories which the tricks fit into.

What you need

You don't need lots of expensive equipment to do magic tricks. All the props in this book are easy to come by and cheap to buy. People are often more impressed by magic done with familiar things.

Use bright new coins rather than older ones. They always look good and attract people's attention.

Playing cards come in lots of different colours and styles. New cards are easiest to handle, as they are quite slippery.

Looking after your props

If you use a lot of props, make sure you know where everything is. Your audience will get bored watching you search for a prop before each trick.

Where to perform

Magic is very versatile. You can do a trick or two wherever you are, as long as you have the things you need. You don't have to be on a stage or in front of a camera.

Keep it a secret

Don't tell anyone how your tricks are done unless they are also real magic enthusiasts. Magicians don't reveal their secrets to anyone except fellow magicians.

MAGIC SKILLS

These two pages explain some magic expressions and techniques which are useful for the tricks. There is also a trick to learn, which uses all of them. Practise Find the Card until you can do it really easily, especially the Magician's Choice part at the end. Then you will find the techniques much easier to use in other tricks.

Face-up, face-down

The instructions for card tricks often tell you to deal cards "face-up" or "face-down". This is because a card has a "face", which shows its suit and value, and a back which is patterned and looks the same as the other cards in the pack.

When you lay a card face-up, you can see its "face". This means you know which card it is.

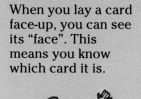

2 When a card is face-down, you cannot tell what it is. You can only see its back.

Cutting cards

When you let volunteers cut the pack you must make sure they cut it this way. Otherwise the sequence of the cards is changed. You could cut the pack once yourself to show a spectator what to do.

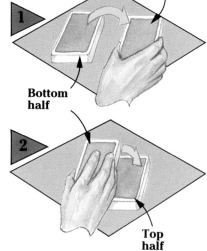

1 Take hold of the top of the pack and lift off roughly half.

Top half

Bottom half

2 Put this half face-down on the table and then complete the cut by putting the other half on top.

Top half

Misdirection

This is a very important skill in magic. It is subtly directing the audience's attention away from what you are doing. Misdirection is built in to the explanations of some tricks, but you need to add it to others yourself. Here are some basic ways of doing it.

Your eyes tell people where to look, so only look at what you want them to notice.

If you want people to think something is in your left hand when it is in your right, watch your left hand with interest and pay no attention to your right hand.

Do every move at the same speed. Changes of pace can make people suspicious.

Repeat a move a few times before doing a sleight (secret move) as part of it. People will not be watching so closely.

When you speak, people look at your face. Talk when you want to divert their attention away from your hands.

Your audience will be suspicious if they see you do something without a good reason. Make sure there is a reason for everything you do. For example, in step 1 of Find the Card when you want to Glimpse the bottom card of the pack, shuffle the cards first. This gives you a reason to square (tidy) the pack and do the Glimpse.

Magician's Choice

This is a useful magic technique which is used in Crosses Across, Double Six and One in Three.* You appear to let your volunteers choose quite freely, but you actually manipulate what they do so they "choose" the one you want them to have.

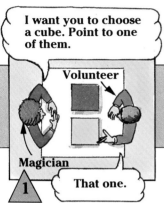

1 "I want you to choose a cube. Point to one of them."
Volunteer
Magician
"That one."

2 "That means you want that one."
"Yes, that's right."

3 "I want you to choose a cube. Point to one of them."
"That one."

So that rules this one out.

4 "So that rules this one out."
"All right."

For example, you have two cubes, one red and one yellow, and you want a volunteer to choose the yellow one. You ask her to point to one.

If she points to the yellow cube, you take the red one away, leaving her with the yellow one, "because she has chosen the yellow one".

Your volunteer is just as likely to point to the one you don't want her to choose. If she does, stay calm and confident, and don't hesitate.

Tell her that she has ruled out the red cube, and take it away. Whichever she points to, you interpret her action to give the result you want.

You can vary this technique to cope with any choice. In One in Three, it is a choice between three things. You will need to do it twice unless your volunteer chooses correctly the first time. If you are brisk and confident, no-one will think of arguing with you.

Find the Card

This is an easy card trick which uses the techniques explained on these two pages. Squaring a pack of cards means tapping the edges on the table to tidy it up after shuffling it, and Glimpsing a card means looking at it quickly without anyone noticing.

Memorize this card.

1 Shuffle the pack, then square it up like this and Glimpse the bottom card. Ask a volunteer to take a card from the pack and memorize it.

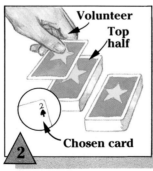

Volunteer
Top half
Chosen card

2 Now cut the pack and ask him to put his card on the top half. Complete the cut, then cut the pack a few more times, saying you are losing his card.

Glimpsed card

3 Look through the pack and take the card you Glimpsed and the two on its right. Put them face-down in the same order, saying you think one is his card.

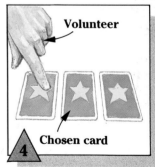

Volunteer
Chosen card

4 Now use Magician's Choice to make the volunteer choose the middle card. Turn it over, thanking him for choosing the same card twice.

Crosses Across is on p38, Double Six p28, and One in Three p47.

All these tricks are quite easy to do and fun to watch. Learn them so that you can do a quick trick whenever you have the right props with you.

Clever Clips

This is a fun way to link two paper clips, using a bank note.* Try changing the positions of the clips, and how sharply you pull, to see how the trick works best.

1 Fold a bank note a third of the way across, then clip the folded third to the rest of the note.

2 Fold the last third of the bank note behind the two thirds you have already clipped together.

3 Clip the last third to the middle layer, with the larger part of the paper clip inside the fold.

4 Hold the ends of the bank note and pull them firmly apart. The paper clips will jump off, linked together.

Cork Twist

This trick sounds quite hard, but with a bit of practice, you will find it really easy. Challenge your friends to do it. They will find it is harder than it looks.

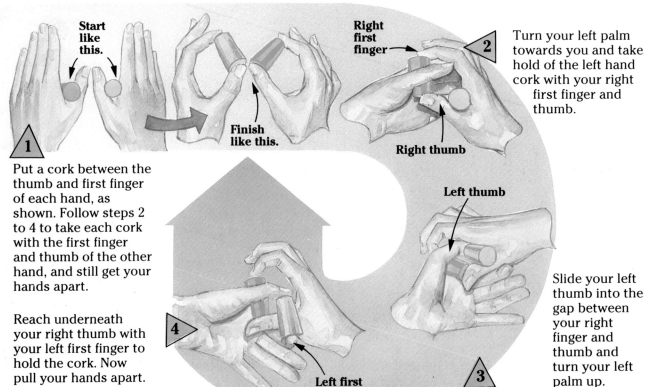

Start like this.

Finish like this.

Right first finger

Right thumb

Left thumb

Left first finger

1 Put a cork between the thumb and first finger of each hand, as shown. Follow steps 2 to 4 to take each cork with the first finger and thumb of the other hand, and still get your hands apart.

Reach underneath your right thumb with your left first finger to hold the cork. Now pull your hands apart.

2 Turn your left palm towards you and take hold of the left hand cork with your right first finger and thumb.

3 Slide your left thumb into the gap between your right finger and thumb and turn your left palm up.

6

* dollar bill in USA.

Vanishing Change

Take some coins from your pocket with your right hand and show them. Say you will make one of them vanish.

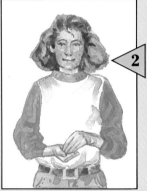

Pretend to take a coin with your left hand. Cup your right hand so the audience cannot see your left fingers.

Put the coins back into your pocket, and show the audience that your right hand is empty.

Pretend to put the coin in your right hand and close it. Turn it over and tap the back with your left hand.

Open your right hand to show that it is empty, and your left hand too. The coin has disappeared.

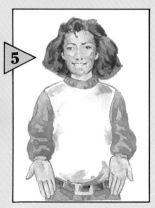

Sixes and Sevens

Take all the sixes and sevens out of a pack of cards. Arrange the sixes and the sevens like this. Do it openly, but do not draw attention to the order you are putting the cards in.

Ask a volunteer to cut the eight cards a few times. Most people do not know that this will not change the order of the cards. Take them back and say you can feel which ones are from each suit.

Cards behind back

To prove it, take the eight cards behind your back. Hold them all in your right hand: the first four between your thumb and first finger, and the others between your first and second fingers.

With your left hand, take the top card of each set of four and drop them face-up on the table. Repeat this with the remaining cards, each time taking the top card from each set.

Take a while to make each pair. The trick will seem harder, and more impressive.

Newspaper Stand

How can two people stand on the same sheet of newspaper and not be able to touch each other?

Put the paper under a door and stand on either side of it.

Squaring the Matches

Set up four matches exactly like this on the table-top. Challenge a friend to make a square by moving only one match.

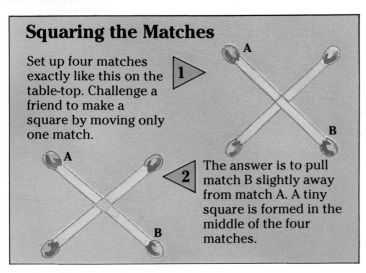

1

A

B

2 The answer is to pull match B slightly away from match A. A tiny square is formed in the middle of the four matches.

A

B

Lift the Bottle

How can you pick up an empty bottle with a drinking straw? This works best with a glass bottle, but make sure you have a hand underneath just in case it falls.

Bend the straw about two-thirds of the way up, and push the bent part into the bottle. It should wedge itself against the side of the bottle, letting you pick it up.

Vanishing Square

This prop is all you need for this trick. First draw a rectangle and 13 evenly-spaced squares in pencil on a piece of cardboard, like this. Then go over them in ink.

Cut out the rectangle, then cut along the red lines dividing A, B and C. Erase the pencil marks. Now you can start the trick.

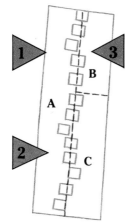

1

3

B

A

C

2

Place the pieces on the table like this. Ask a volunteer to count the squares. There are 13.

Rearrange the pieces, swapping C and B. Ask the volunteer to count again. This time there are only 12 squares. One has vanished.

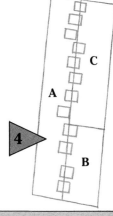

C

A

4

B

Making an Entrance

This is a silly joke which you can use when coming into a room. It works best with a door which opens away from you.

1 Pop your head around the door and say "Hello", holding the edge of the door with one hand.

2 Now reach behind your head with the other hand. Grab your neck and pull yourself back behind the door, acting surprised.

Pull the Cork

Push a tight-fitting cork into the neck of a plastic bottle. Then push it right inside. How can you get it out without breaking the bottle?

1 To do this, take a handkerchief or a thin tea-towel and push one end inside the bottle. Shake it so the cork falls against the handkerchief.

2 Now pull the handkerchief slowly out of the bottle. It should pull the cork out, too. It might be a bit stiff at the end, but keep pulling.

Dice Roll

Turned over

Rolled again

Magician's sum
6 + 5 + 4 + 7 = 22

1 2+6+5 = 13

Turn your back, asking a friend to roll three dice and add up the numbers on them.

2 13 + 5 = 18

Ask him to turn one of the dice upside-down and add its new number to his total.

3 18 + 4 = 22

Now ask him to roll this dice again and add this third number to the total.

4

Turn back and silently add up the dice. Add seven to get your friend's total.

Three Dice Trick

This trick looks impressive and people will be unable to copy it. You need to moisten your first finger and thumb before you start. Make sure no-one sees you do this.

Hold three dice between your thumb and first finger, like this. Release the pressure on the dice a little.

1

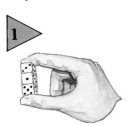

This lets the middle dice fall while the other two stay between your fingers, as they will stick to them slightly.

2

Tower of Dice

 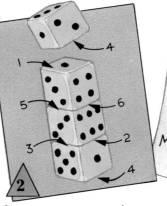 

Volunteer's sum:
4 + 1 = 5
+6 = 11
+5 = 16
+2 = 18
+3 = 21
+4 = 25
Magician's sum:
28 - 3 = 25

1

Turn your back, asking a volunteer to make a tower by putting four dice on top of each other, with the numbers in any position. Turn, glance at the top dice, and turn your back again.

2

Say you can remember some of the numbers you saw, and ask her to add up the numbers on the faces you did not see: the bottom of the top dice and the top and bottom of the other three.

3

Turn back and announce the total of the hidden faces: you will be right if you subtract the number on the top dice from 28, as the opposite faces of a dice always add up to 7.

Dice Count

2 × 2 = 4
4 + 5 = 9
9 × 5 = 45

1 45 + 3 = 48

With your back turned so you cannot see the dice, ask someone to roll two dice and double the number on one of them. Then he should add five, multiply the answer by five, and add the number on the other dice.

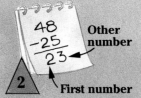

48
−25
23

Other number

2

First number

Ask the volunteer his total. Subtract 25 from it. You will get a two-figure number, made up of the two numbers he rolled, first the one he used first and then the other.

Static Trick

Take a fairly thick coin and balance it on its edge. Now balance a match across the top of the coin. How can you move the match off the coin without touching either of them?

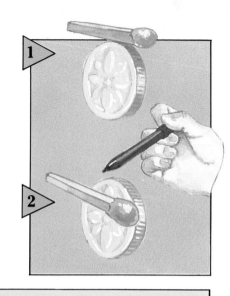

Rub a plastic pen on your hair or something made of nylon. Hold the pen close to the match. The static electricity on the pen makes the match move and fall off the coin.

Three Coin Trick

Put three coins in a row, with the middle one closer to the coin on one side than the other. Set them up slowly and carefully. Which coins are furthest apart? A lot of people will say A and B, but the answer is really A and C.

Double Your Money

Wait a second, then say seriously that you can really increase it. Fold it twice more, unfold it and show it to them "in creases".

1 Show a bank note, saying that you can double it. Fold it in half, and show it "doubled". The audience should groan.

2

Coin Circle

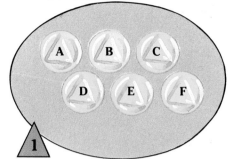

1

How can you move these coins to make a circle? You are only allowed three moves, and each coin you move must end up between two other coins.

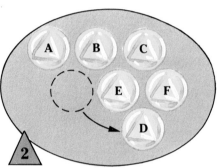

2

First move D between E and F.

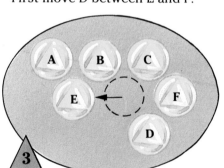

3

Then move E between A and B.

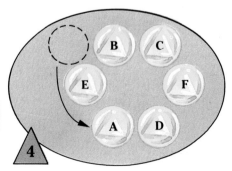

4

Lastly, move A between E and D.

Coin Hit

Put three coins touching each other in a row. How can you move coin A away from coins B and C? You are allowed to move but not touch coin A, touch but not move coin B, and touch and move C.

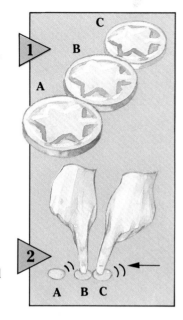

Hold B down with a finger, and knock coin C against B. Coin A will move away from B.

Catch it if You Can

Hold a bank note like this. Ask a volunteer to position his hand halfway down the note, ready to catch it when you drop it. Bet him he cannot catch it before it hits the ground. Almost no-one will be quick enough.

Volunteer's hand must not be touching the note.

Magician

Four in a Row

Make an L-shape with six coins, four down and three across. How can you move one coin so that both rows have four coins in them?

Put coin A on top of coin B.

One Note or Two

These instructions tell you how to fold a bank note so that it looks like two. You could use it to joke about how rich you are, or to trick your friends.

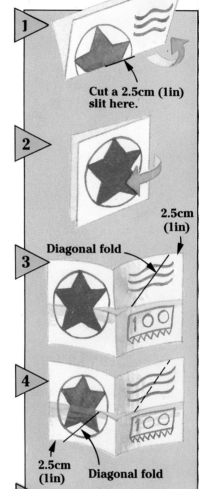

Fold the bank note in half lengthways away from you, and cut a slit about 2.5cm (1in) long in the middle of the fold.

Cut a 2.5cm (1in) slit here.

Now unfold the note and fold it in half widthways, without turning it over.

2.5cm (1in)

Unfold it again and make a diagonal fold towards you from one end of the slit to about 2.5cm (1in) from the end of the note.

Diagonal fold

Then make another fold like this from the other end of the slit to the other long edge of the note.

2.5cm (1in) **Diagonal fold**

Folding the note along the lengthways crease, take hold of both short ends of the note and push them towards the middle.

Push **Push**

Now fold the note in half along the diagonal creases. It will look like two notes when you hold it up like this.

11

SELF-WORKING CARD TRICKS

Self-working tricks rely on certain cards being in certain positions in the pack. You need to set them up before you start, so your audience doesn't suspect anything.

Remember not to shuffle the cards by accident. Although these tricks are not difficult, they are really effective when performed smoothly.

Rising Cards

In this trick, you put two cards in the middle of a pack, and make them appear to rise to the top. To prepare, put the seven of hearts and eight of clubs on top of the pack.

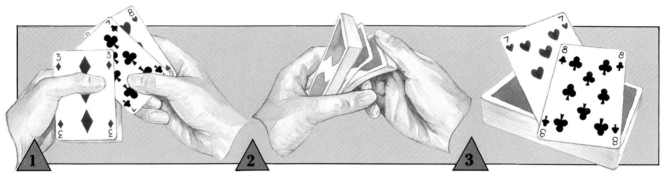

1 Take the seven of clubs and eight of hearts from the pack, pretending to choose then at random. Show them briefly to the audience, without naming them. Then put them into the middle of the pack.

2 Riffle the edges of the pack with your fingers, saying this will help the chosen cards rise to the top. Then put the cards down and tap the top of the pack, saying the cards should have arrived.

3 Turn over the top two cards: the seven of hearts and eight of clubs. These are not the cards you chose, but as you did not name them and they look very similar, the audience will not notice the difference.

Matching Pairs

Here you predict when a volunteer will tell you to stop dealing. Have the nine of clubs on top of the pack and the three of diamonds on the bottom.

1 Say you will pick two cards to match the ones he chooses when he stops you dealing. Take the three of hearts and nine of spades. Lay them face-down, without showing them.

2 Start dealing the cards face-down, asking your volunteer to say "Stop". When he does, lay the three of hearts face-up on the dealt cards, and put the rest of the pack on top of the three of hearts.

3 Now start dealing from the top of the pack again, asking the volunteer when to stop. This time put the nine of spades face-up on top of the dealt cards and the rest of the pack on top again.

4 Remind the volunteer that you chose your cards before dealing. Take the three of hearts and nine of spades out of the pack with the card above each of them. Reveal the matching pairs.

Double Prediction

Start with the ace of spades, two of hearts, four of diamonds and eight of clubs in this order on top of the pack. By adding up the values of some or all of these cards you can equal the value of any card (king=13=1+4+8). Also, each of the four cards matches a suit.

Take the four cards off the pack and put them in your pocket, keeping them squared to hide how many you are taking. Tell a spectator you have predicted the card he will choose. Ask him to name it.

Take out the cards which make up the named card's value. To predict its suit, show the card of the same suit last, even if it is not needed for the value. The cards shown make up the king of clubs.

Finding the Fours

To prepare for this trick, put the four fours 10th, 20th, 30th and 40th in the pack.

Ask a volunteer for a number between 10 and 20. If he says 16, deal 16 cards face-down. Say "16 is 1 and 6. 1 and 6 is 7", and deal six cards back onto the pack. Leave the seventh face-down on the table beside the other cards.

Ask for another number between 10 and 20. If it is 12 this time, deal 12 cards face-down. Say "12 is 1 and 2, 1 and 2 is 3", and deal two cards back onto the pack. Put the third card face-down as before.

Repeat this process twice more. Remind your volunteer that he could have chosen any numbers between 10 and 20. Now turn over the four cards. They are all fours.

Weighing Cards

Give any 13 red and 13 black cards to someone to shuffle. Start dealing them face-down, counting silently. Ask the volunteer to say "Stop". When she does, you can tell how many more or less red cards you have than she has black cards.

If you stopped before the 13th card, subtract the number of cards you dealt from 13. You have that many more red cards than she has black. If you stopped after 13, subtract 13 from the number you dealt. You have that many less red cards than she has black.

While you are working out the answer in your head, pretend to weigh your cards, as if this is the trick. Give your answer and ask the volunteer to check whether you are right by counting the number of red and black cards in the two hands.

FUN WITH FOOD

Sticky Sugar

For this trick you need two lumps of sugar, one of which has a smear of butter on one side. You could set up a bowl of sugar-lumps on the table with the buttered one ready in it so you would appear to be taking two lumps at random.

Butter

1 Hold one lump between the forefinger and thumb of each hand, with the buttered side hidden.

2 Rub one lump against your sleeve, saying you will stick them together with static electricity.

3 Turn the buttered lump around and stick the lumps together. Hold them up to show everyone.

4 To finish the trick, get rid of the evidence by eating both lumps of sugar.

Balancing Grape

1 Start with your first finger pointing upwards, secretly holding a cocktail stick* behind it with your thumb. Keep the point just below the tip of your finger.

2 Tell the audience that you will balance a grape on your finger. Push the grape onto the cocktail stick, pretending to position it on the end of your finger.

3 Move your hand as if it is difficult to keep the grape balanced, and pretend to concentrate hard. Keep your palm towards you to hide the cocktail stick.

4 To finish, take the grape off the cocktail stick and give it to someone in the audience to try the trick. While no-one is watching, put the stick in your pocket.

Take a Bite

1 Hold a coin between your first and second fingers, like this, and have a piece you have bitten off a white mint in your mouth.

Coin

2 Pick up a white mug in the same hand. Hold the coin squeezed between your fingers and the mug, but resting against your first finger. No-one should see the coin.

14   **** You could use a toothpick instead.***

Bouncing Apple

You need to be sitting at a table facing sideways to do this, so it is a good dinner-time trick. If you time the actions properly, as well as stamping your foot, it looks and sounds as if you really have bounced the apple on the floor.

1 Hold an apple in your hand and pretend to throw it at the floor, moving your arm below the table top. Try it with a ball to get the move right.

Stamp your foot.

2 As the apple goes below the table top, stamp your foot. Toss the apple into the air at once, still keeping your hand below the table top.

3 Bring your hand above the table to catch the apple as it falls again. A good finishing touch is to prove it is a real apple by biting it.

Raise the mug to your mouth. Press your second finger hard against the mug and lift your first finger slightly. The coin will slide off your finger and clink.

3 Coin clinks on mug.

Pull the mug away and spit out the piece of mint, looking astonished. Keep the mug tilted towards you or people will see you have not taken a bite out of it.

4

Now worriedly rub the rim of the mug with your other hand. Look relieved and tilt the mug away from you to show you have "mended" it.

5

Slicing a Banana

Move the stick inside the skin.

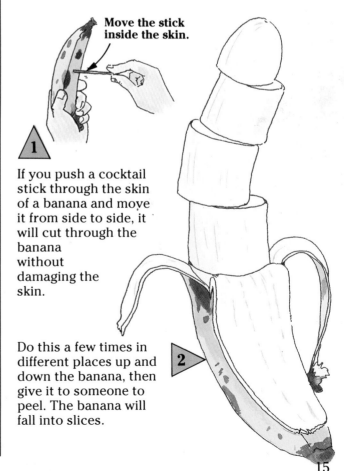

1 If you push a cocktail stick through the skin of a banana and move it from side to side, it will cut through the banana without damaging the skin.

2 Do this a few times in different places up and down the banana, then give it to someone to peel. The banana will fall into slices.

Magic Matchbox

Take the tray out of a box of matches and cut a piece off the end, about three-quarters of the way along.

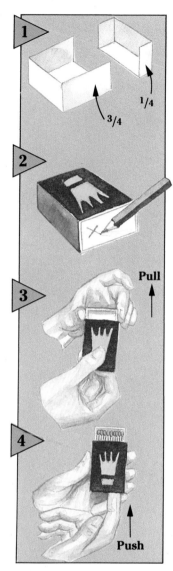

1

1/4

3/4

2

Put the pieces of tray back into the cover, and mark the long end to recognize it. Put the matches back in, with their heads at the marked end.

To start the trick, hold the box upright. Push the unmarked end a little and pull out the long end of the tray. It looks as if the matchbox is empty.

Pull

3

Push in the marked end, then open the box again by pushing on the short end. The matches have appeared in the box.

4

Push

Matchbox Challenge

This stunt is difficult, but if you practise a lot, it will become easier. Then you can challenge your friends, and they will find it much harder than it looks.

Empty the tray of a matchbox and stand it on one end. Lay the cover down in front of the tray.

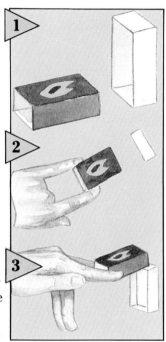

1

Resting the tips of your second and third fingers on the table, grip the tray between your first and little fingers.

2

Keeping your second and third fingers on the table, lift the cover and put it on top of the tray.

3

Lift the Matches

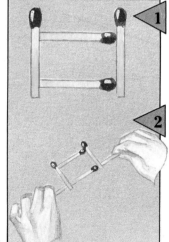

1

Set up four matches on the table as in the picture. How can you lift them all off the table, using two other matches?

2

Press the two matches against the uprights, exactly opposite the ends of one of the cross-bars. Start lifting them slowly and carefully off the table. It will work when you get the positions exactly right.

Be careful not to strike a match by accident when you are doing any of these tricks.

Tip

Keep the Magic Matchbox in a special place, or you might try to use it for another trick. This could ruin that trick as well as giving away the secret of Magic Matchbox. Always make sure you know where your props are.

Escaping Match

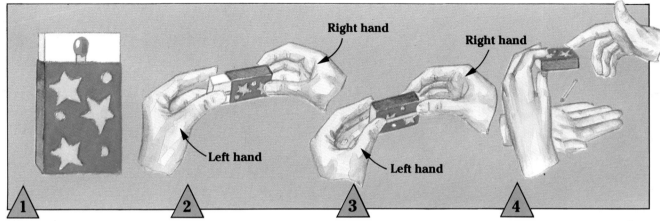

1 Before you start, slide a match between the cover of a full matchbox and the bottom of the tray. Make sure this match faces the same way as the matches in the box.

2 In front of the audience, open the box and remove the cover with your right hand. Keep hold of the tray and the match underneath it with your left hand.

3 Carefully replace the cover, holding the end of the match with your left thumb. Make sure the match stays outside the cover, and hold it there with your thumb.

4 Hold the box over a friend's hand and give it a tap. Let the match drop into her hand. It looks as if it has escaped through the bottom of the matchbox.

Match Glass Puzzle

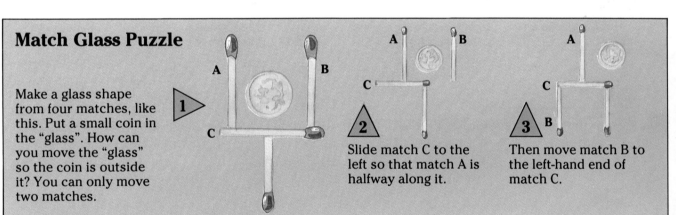

Make a glass shape from four matches, like this. Put a small coin in the "glass". How can you move the "glass" so the coin is outside it? You can only move two matches.

2 Slide match C to the left so that match A is halfway along it.

3 Then move match B to the left-hand end of match C.

Pyramid of Matches

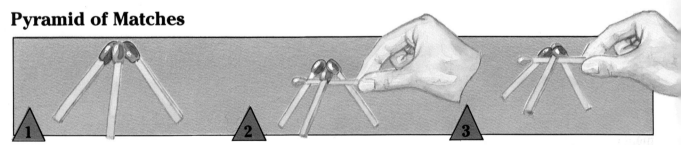

1 Glue two matches together by the ends and lean a third against them so they stand up like this. How can you lift the three matches off the table with another match?

2 Put the fourth match between the two stuck matches and the balanced one. Push the stuck matches slightly so that the balanced one falls between them onto the fourth match.

3 By lifting the fourth match you can trap the three matches together and lift them all off the table, still in the pyramid shape they formed standing on the table.

17

CARD DISCOVERIES

These are tricks where a volunteer chooses a card and replaces it in the pack. Then the magician finds the chosen card without having seen it.

Single Reverse

Cards behind back

Tip

1 Ask a spectator to take a card and memorize it. Face away from him, saying you don't want to see the card. Turn the pack over and turn the top card upside-down, so the pack has two "tops".

2 Turn back, take the spectator's card and push it into the pack. Do it slowly, so the audience does not see the cards are upside-down. Say you are trying to memorize the card's position.

3 Put your hands behind you, saying you will try to find the card. Turn the top card over again, and turn the pack over. Spread the cards face-down on the table. The spectator's card will be face-up.

Try to keep the cards squared when you do a Reverse trick. If someone sees the edge of a card's face, they may realize the cards are upside-down.

Double Reverse

This is a more complicated version of the Single Reverse. Ask a volunteer to shuffle the pack and give you roughly half. Ask him to look at a card from his half and put it face-down on the table. Say you will do the same, and turn your back.

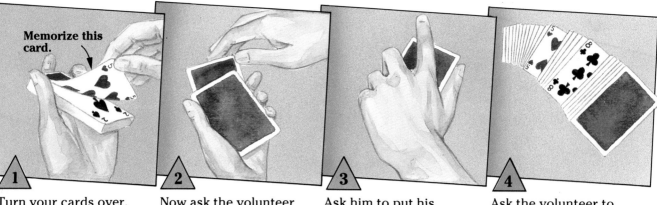

Memorize this card.

1 Turn your cards over, memorize the top card and turn it upside-down. Take another card and pretend to memorize it. Turn back and put it face-down on the table.

2 Now ask the volunteer to copy exactly what you do. Holding your cards as if you are about to deal them, slide his chosen card into them, without looking at it.

3 Ask him to put his cards on the table, pointing to a place with your left hand. Turn your hand as you point, reversing your cards again. Put them on top of his.

4 Ask the volunteer to name his card. Name the card you turned upside-down, and spread the pack face-down on the table. Your chosen cards will both be face-up.

The Card in Mind

In this trick, you find a card which a volunteer has not even taken from the pack. If you don't get the cards you need in step 1, ask the volunteer to shuffle the pack and deal again.

Memorize this card.

1 Ask a volunteer to deal you 15 cards. Take a spade, a heart, a diamond and two clubs, and show them arranged like this. Ask him to memorize one of the cards, remembering the last card yourself.

2 Put your five cards on the pack and the other ten on top of them. Now put the top five cards in the middle of the pack, then the bottom five, then the new top five. Your five cards are on top again.

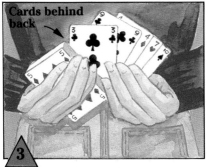

Cards behind back

3 Hold the pack behind you and ask the volunteer to name his chosen card. You know the last card of the top five and the order of the suits, so you can pick out his card. Produce the chosen card.

Last Card Left

Chosen card · **Bottom half** · **Top half** · **Glimpsed card on bottom**

1 First shuffle the pack a few times. Then tap it on the table to square it up, turning the cards slightly towards you to Glimpse the bottom card.

2 Ask a spectator to take a card and memorize it. Cut the pack on the table. Ask him to lay his card on the top half. Then put the bottom half on top.

3 Have the pack cut a few times, then pick up the cards to look for his. When you find the card you Glimpsed, cut the pack so that it is on the bottom again.

Put 21 cards behind the others.

4 Say you cannot find his card. Look through the pack again, silently counting 21 cards. Put these cards on top of the pack, saying you will have to find his card another way.

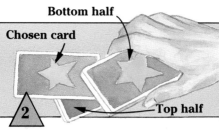

5 Deal the pack face-down into two piles, dealing the first card to the spectator, then alternately. Ask him to look through his half of the pack for his card. He will not find it.

Chosen card

6 Deal your pile into two, dealing the first card to the spectator as before. Ask him to look again. Repeat this until you only have one card left. This card is the one he chose.

PAPER TRICKS

These tricks all involve cutting, tearing, or folding paper. You use a playing card for one and a postcard for another. Think before cutting things up, especially playing cards: use a joker or a card from a pack which is already incomplete.

Expanding Card

Take a playing card, or a piece of card the same size. Bet a friend that you can put your head through it. Fold it in half widthways and cut a slit, like this.

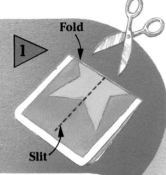

1

Fold

Slit

2 Unfold the card and cut short slits from the long edges towards the centre slit. If you cut through to the centre slit, you will need to start on a new card.

Short slits

3 Cut more short slits between the others, starting at the centre slit and cutting as close to the edges as possible.

Cut from centre slit.

4 You can now open up a hole in the card big enough to put your head through. The more slits you cut, the bigger the hole will be.

Linking Card

Make this puzzle in secret so no-one sees how to do it. Unless you tear or cut something, you can only take the rings off the card by bending it as in step 4.

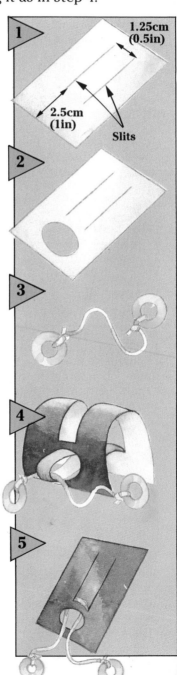

1 Cut two parallel slits lengthways down the middle of a postcard, about 1.25cm (0.5in) apart, leaving 2.5cm (1in) uncut at one end.

1.25cm (0.5in)

2.5cm (1in)

Slits

2 Now cut a hole in the 2.5cm (1in) space at the end of the card, slightly wider than the strip between the slits.

3 Cut two cardboard rings just too wide to fit through the hole. Tie them together with a piece of string about 25cm (10in) long.

4 Bend the card and pull the strip through the hole. Loop the rings onto the strip by feeding the string through.

5 Straighten the card again. It will look like this. Now you can challenge someone to take the rings and string off the card.

Make a Movie

Here is a way to make a simple moving picture. When you know how to do it, try other pictures.

10cm (4in)

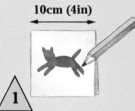

1

Cut a strip of paper 20cm by 10cm (8in by 4in). Fold it in half widthways and draw this picture on the top.

2

Draw this picture on the bottom flap, so that it lies right underneath the picture on the top flap.

3

Roll the top flap tightly around a pencil and hold the paper by the fold at the top. Move the pencil up and down to roll and unroll the top flap. The picture moves.

Paper Tree

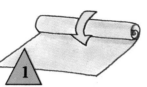

1

Take a sheet of fairly thin coloured paper or newspaper and roll it up tightly, starting from one of the short sides. Hold one end with an elastic band.

Elastic band

2

Cut through all the layers to about halfway down the roll. Do this in three or four places, always starting at the same end.

3

Take hold of the middle layer and pull it gently but firmly out of the roll. Don't worry if it tears. The tree will still look fine.

For a brown tree with green leaves, stick three sheets of green paper together with a brown one at the end. Roll them with the brown one outside.

Paper Tear

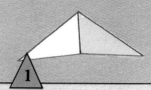

1

Tear a little triangle from the margin of a newspaper and fold it in half.

2

Crinkle one half of the triangle and fold it so that it stands out.

3

Moisten the flat half and stick it on the wallpaper. It will look like a tear.

4

Be careful who you try this joke on. Not everyone will be amused.

Instant Change

This is a very quick trick. The audience see you pass a small coin from one hand to the other, but as you do so, it seems to change into a much larger coin.

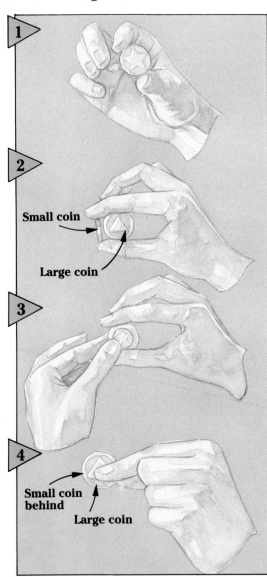

Hold a small coin by its rim between the thumb and first finger of your right hand.

1

Hold a larger coin behind the first, at right angles to it, so that the audience cannot see it behind the smaller coin.

2

Small coin

Large coin

Move your left hand over to take the coins. Your left thumb pushes the small coin so that it turns and is hidden beside the larger one.

3

Take the larger coin with the small one behind it between your left first finger and thumb and show it to the audience.

4

Small coin behind

Large coin

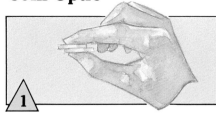

1

Hold a coin in your right hand and ask a volunteer to hold her hands out, palms up. Ask her to close her hands over the coin on the count of three.

Coin Optic

1

Hold two coins flat on top of each other between your thumb and forefinger like this, sideways to the audience. Say you will make an extra coin by rubbing them together.

Turning Coins

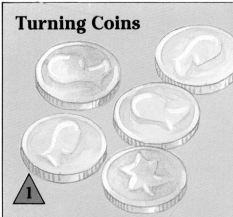

1

Throw some coins onto the table, and note silently whether there are an odd or even number of heads.

Tip

In tricks like Instant Change, coins can "talk", or clink when they are not supposed to. The only way to avoid this is to practise handling the coins smoothly.

2

Raise your hand above your head and bring it down to touch her hands with the coin. Count one. Do this again and count two as you touch her palms.

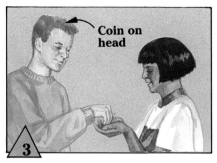

Coin on head

3

The third time you raise your hand above your head, leave the coin on top of your head. Then bring down your empty hand to hers, counting three.

4

Show her the coin has gone, then say you will re-produce it if she keeps her hands still. Tilt your head forward. The coin will fall into her hands.

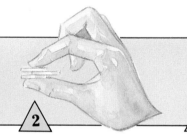

2

Rub the coins quickly backwards and forwards against each other. It looks as if there are three coins, not two.

3

Learn to do this with a coin squeezed between the fleshy base of your thumb and palm. This is called a Classic Palm.

4

Then if a spectator says it is only an optical illusion, you can throw three coins down onto the table.

Tip

It is easier to do this trick on someone who is shorter than you.

2

Ask a volunteer to turn the coins over as many times as she likes, but always two at a time, never singly. Turn your back.

3

Ask the volunteer to cover one coin. When you turn back, you can predict whether the hidden coin is a head or a tail.

4

If the number of heads was odd before and is still odd, or was even before and is still even, then the hidden coin is a tail.

5

If the number of heads was odd before and is now even, or was even before and is now odd, then the hidden coin is a head.

TRICKS WITH HANDKERCHIEFS

Knots and Crosses

Bet a friend that you can tie a knot in a handkerchief without letting go of the ends.

1. Stretch the handkerchief diagonally and lay it on the table in front of you.

2. Let go of the handkerchief and cross your arms. Now take hold of the ends of the handkerchief.

3. Slowly unfold your arms, still holding the ends of the handkerchief.

4. By unfolding your arms you transfer the "knot" in them to the handkerchief.

Funny Face

This is a good joke to do with glasses or sun-glasses. You could use it as an introduction to a series of tricks with handkerchiefs.

Lay a handkerchief over your face, and put on your glasses over the handkerchief. Put something in your mouth as well to make it look funnier.

Tip

Make sure your handkerchiefs are clean and ironed. Shabby props make you look like a bad magician even before you start.

Straight Through

1. Make a circle by bending your left fingers to meet your thumb. Drape a handkerchief over this hand.

2. Push your right first finger down into the centre of the handkerchief, to make a well in it.

You are making a channel through the handkerchief.

3. Now secretly part your left fingers and thumb slightly and bring your middle finger in beside your first finger.

Loose Ends

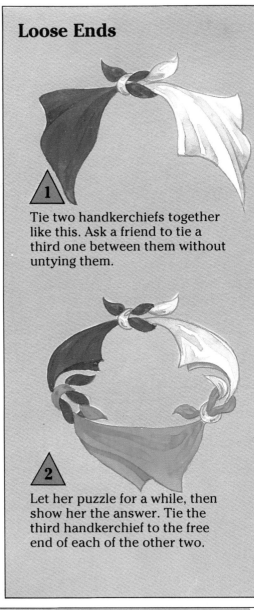

Tie two handkerchiefs together like this. Ask a friend to tie a third one between them without untying them.

Let her puzzle for a while, then show her the answer. Tie the third handkerchief to the free end of each of the other two.

Hold a handkerchief by the middle and pull it up through your right fist. Grip it between your right thumb and forefinger and curl the other fingers loosely around it.

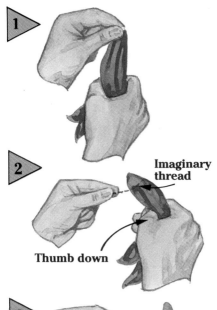

Pretend to tie a thread to the handkerchief, and to tug it with your left hand, moving your right thumb down the handkerchief a little. It moves as if it is being pulled.

Imaginary thread

Thumb down

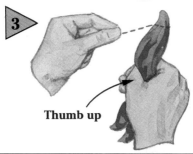

Bring your left hand a little closer to your right and move your thumb back up the handkerchief. It moves as if the thread has been slackened. Repeat a few times.

Thumb up

Tip

Think about what to do with your "invisible prop" at the end of the trick. It looks bad if you just forget it. Pretend to untie the thread or break it and throw it away.

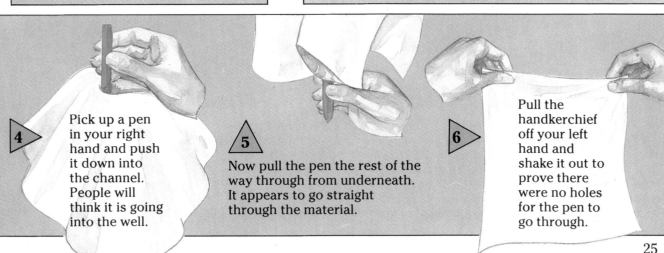

Pick up a pen in your right hand and push it down into the channel. People will think it is going into the well.

Now pull the pen the rest of the way through from underneath. It appears to go straight through the material.

Pull the handkerchief off your left hand and shake it out to prove there were no holes for the pen to go through.

GAMBLERS' TRICKS

Cheats and gamblers invented many of the techniques now used in card tricks, as ways of improving their chances of winning. The tricks below show the kinds of things gamblers did. You could present them as a demonstration.

Gambler's tip

Like a gambler playing cards, a magician must learn to control his expression. It is very important that his face should not tell people when he is up to something.

Dealing Fives

Say one way gamblers can improve their luck is by dealing themselves the cards they want. Here you demonstrate this, dealing three fives to the audience every time you deal.

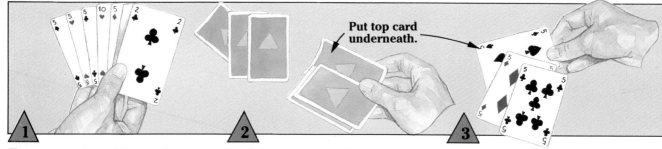

Put top card underneath.

1
To prepare the trick, set the pack up exactly like this, with a black five on top, then a red five, the other black five, any card and then the other red five.

2
Deal the top six cards to your audience and yourself in turn, starting with the audience. Put your top card under the other two and put all three cards back on the pack.

3
Turn the other hand face-up, then slide the top card under the other two. Show the audience that this hand contains one red five between two black fives.

Bottom and Centre Dealing

Here you show how cards can be dealt from the bottom of the pack, and then pretend to take others from the middle of the pack to get a winning hand. To prepare, secretly set up the pack with the two, three, four and five of spades on top.

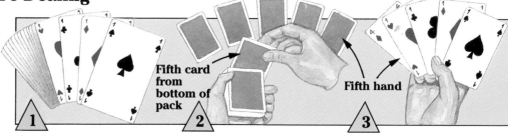

Fifth card from bottom of pack

Fifth hand

1
Openly put the four aces at the bottom of the pack, with the ace of spades right at the bottom. Say you will now demonstrate bottom dealing.

2
Start dealing five hands. Deal the first four cards normally, but the fifth from the bottom of the pack. Repeat this until each hand has five cards.

3
Turn the fifth hand over. It contains the four aces. Now put all the hands back on top of the pack, saying you will show off centre dealing.

Tip

Do not worry if your hands seem too small for the cards you are using. If you keep practising, you will overcome the problem.

4

Put the cards back on the pack and deal again. Even though you deal alternately to the audience and yourself, the same three cards seem to come back to the audience every time.

Many gamblers' tricks involve a lot of dealing. Try to keep things moving so you don't bore your audience.

4

Deal another five hands of five cards. Deal suspiciously fast every time you come to the fifth hand, but actually deal all the cards normally.

5

Turn over the fifth hand again for a surprise ending. The audience may be expecting the four aces again, but it is the ace to five of spades.

Gambler's Bluff

A good gambler's voice will not give away his cards. Here you pretend to recognize a chosen card from the tone of a volunteer's voice. To prepare, put the four aces aside and secretly put six hearts on top of the pack and six on the bottom.

Volunteer

1

Ask a volunteer to deal the 48 cards into six piles, take a card from the middle of a pile and memorize it.

2

Then ask her to put her card on top of any pile, and put the other piles on top and underneath.

3

Let her cut the pack a few times, then ask her to deal the cards face-up, naming them as she deals them.

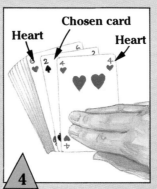

Heart · Chosen card · Heart

4

Stop her when you hear a card between two hearts. It is her card. Pretend you knew from her voice.

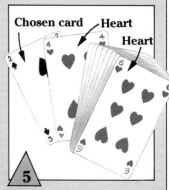

Chosen card · Heart · Heart

5

If you miss it, ask her to deal again. It could be the first card in the pack if the second is a single heart.

PAPER AND PENCIL FUN

Pencil Twist

This is quite a difficult puzzle at first, but it soon becomes very easy. When you can do it easily, show it to your friends once and bet that they will not be able to do it.

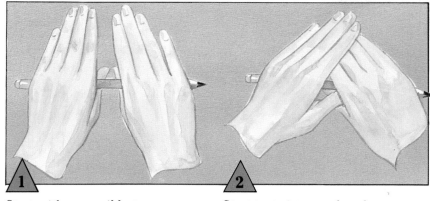

1 Start with a pencil between your thumbs and palms, like this. The puzzle is to move the pencil to on top of your hands without letting go.

2 Start to twist your hands, so that your right thumb goes under your left thumb, and your right fingers go under your left fingers.

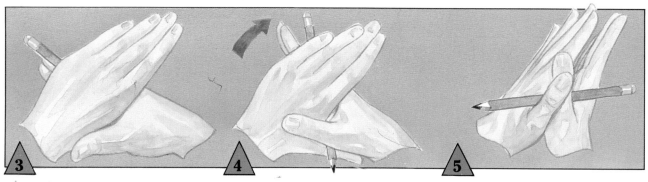

3 Twist your right hand down, so the base of your left thumb is between your right first finger and thumb, with the pencil across your left palm.

4 Now twist your right hand so that your first finger goes across your left palm and fingers, pushing the pencil upwards as it turns.

5 Twist your right hand until your palms are together. Now uncross your thumbs. The pencil is on top of your hands instead of underneath.

Double Six

6 has only one torn edge.

1 Cut a strip of paper and write the numbers 1-10 in ten equal sections on the strip. Make sure that 6 and 9 are at the ends, and the "9" is an upside-down 6.

2 Tear the paper into ten pieces, and make two face-down piles of five. Put the 6 in one pile and the "9" in the other. (They are the pieces with only one torn edge).

3 Take another piece of paper and write SIX on it, then fold it up and put it aside. Say you have predicted which number a volunteer will choose.

Tip

If you act surprised or pleased at a trick, your audience will enjoy it more. But if you seem indifferent, they may not be impressed either.

You could do this trick indoors or under an umbrella. Firmly hold a piece of paper with a pencil underneath it, like this. Now move your thumb very slightly. It will make a sound like a raindrop falling.

Each time you move your thumb, look up for the drips, holding the paper as if to catch them. If you are good at bluffing, you can fool people that there is a leak.

1

2

Pencil under here

Disappearing Pencil

1

Holding a coin in one hand, pick up a pencil in the other. Raise the pencil to beside your head, saying you will make the coin disappear.

2

Lower the pencil to tap the coin in an exaggerated magic gesture. Do this a few times, looking worried when the coin does not disappear.

3

Raise the pencil a last time and stick it behind your ear. Lower your hand to touch the coin, and look surprised that the pencil has gone.

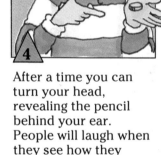

4

After a time you can turn your head, revealing the pencil behind your ear. People will laugh when they see how they have been fooled.

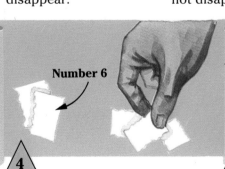

Number 6

4

Ask your volunteer to choose one pile and destroy it. Divide the other pile into two, making sure the 6 is in the pile of two pieces.

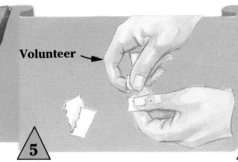

Volunteer

5

Now ask her to touch a pile. Whichever it is, ask her to destroy the pile of three pieces.* Lay the last two face-down and ask her to pick up one of them.

Magician

Volunteer

6

If she takes the 6, reveal your prediction. If she takes the other piece, tell her to destroy it. Then ask to see the last piece and reveal your prediction.

Use Magician's Choice for these two steps - see p5.

COIN JUGGLING

Hand Catch

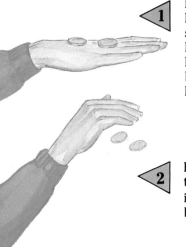

▷**1** Hold your arm out, level with your shoulder, with your hand palm-down. Put two coins on the back of your hand, like this.

▷**2** Flick your hand up, tossing the coins into the air. Quickly bend your arm.

▷**3** Now straighten your arm, moving your hand forward to catch the coins before they fall.

Elbow Catch

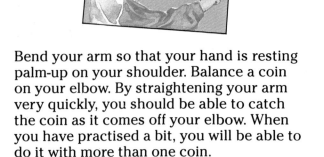

Bend your arm so that your hand is resting palm-up on your shoulder. Balance a coin on your elbow. By straightening your arm very quickly, you should be able to catch the coin as it comes off your elbow. When you have practised a bit, you will be able to do it with more than one coin.

Balancing Coin

In this trick, you balance a coin on your right first finger. It appears to be attached to your finger as you slap it into the palm of your other hand and then bring it back again.

▷**1** First show the audience a fairly large coin balanced on the end of your right first finger.

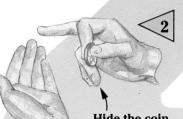

2 As you turn your hand to slap the coin down, hold the coin between your first finger and thumb, like this.

Hide the coin with your other fingers.

▷**3** At the same time stretch out your right middle finger, and slap it down into your left palm.

◁**4** Reverse the steps, and show the audience the coin still balanced on your right first finger.

Coin Roll

This is a very difficult flourish (an eye-catching effect), which needs lots of practice. Once you can do it quickly and confidently, it looks really impressive, as if the coin is tripping across your hand all on its own. Although you can do it with either hand, use the one you write with at first, as it will be your stronger hand.

1 Hold a fairly large coin against the first joint of your first finger with your thumb, like this.

2 Tip the coin onto the back of your first finger with your thumb. Pull it between your first and second fingers with your second finger.

3 Now tip the coin onto the back of your second finger with your first finger.

4 Roll the coin over onto your third finger, using your second finger.

5 Now tip the coin into the gap between your third and little fingers. Bring your thumb across under your little finger and catch the coin as it slides down.

6 With your thumb, squeeze the coin flat underneath your fingers. Slide it back across and bring it up beside your first finger to start again.

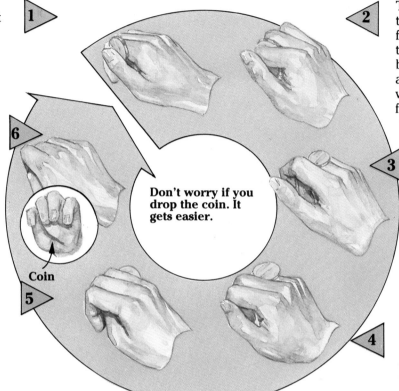

Coin

Don't worry if you drop the coin. It gets easier.

Coin Roll Vanish

When you have mastered the Coin Roll and you can do it without thinking, try this. The effect is quite easy to do, and adds a magic emphasis to the flourish.

1 Do the Coin Roll steps 1-5, and when the coin slides down between your fingers, pretend to take it with your other hand. Curl your fingers to hide what you are doing.

Watch this hand.

2 Casually drop the hand with the coin to your side, hiding the coin. Put your empty hand in your pocket, watching it as you do it. Pretend to leave the coin in your pocket.

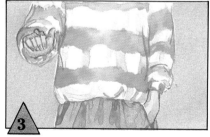

3 As this hand goes into your pocket, move the other hand forward, doing step 6 of the Coin Roll, and start the Roll again. It looks as if you have produced another coin.

ELASTIC BAND TRICKS

An elastic band is the only prop you need to do the tricks on these two pages. If you twist them cleverly, you can make elastic bands do surprising things.

Snap

This effect is hard to get right at first, but well worth the effort. In the trick, the audience hears you snap a band and sees the break, but you immediately mend it "by magic". Practise a lot until you can do steps 1-5 really quickly and easily.

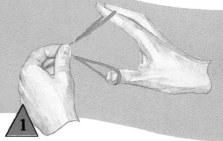

1 Loop the band around your right thumb and first finger. Take hold of the middle of the loop with your left thumb and first finger.

2 Pull your hands apart. Bring your right thumb and first finger together, letting the loop from your thumb slip onto your finger.

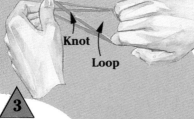

Knot
Loop

3 Put the rest of your fingers into the right hand side of the figure eight you have made. Stretch it around them so it looks like a single thickness.

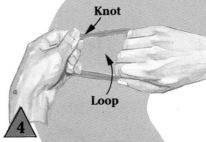

Knot
Loop

4 Now put your left fingers into the loop, taking hold of the knot between your left first finger and thumb. Keep the band stretched tightly.

5 Take your right first finger out of the loop. Then hold the band beside your left thumb and first finger with your right thumb and first finger.

6 Still keeping the double loop stretched to look like a single loop, pull your hands apart. The band will make a convincing snapping noise.

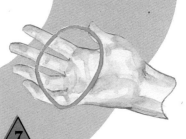

7 Show the "snapped" band for a moment, then gather it into your right hand. Blow into your hand and pull out the "mended" elastic band.

Through Your Thumb

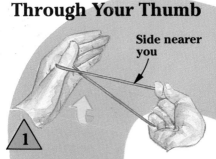

Side nearer you

1 Loop a band around your left thumb. Twist the band so that the side nearer to you goes over the other side.

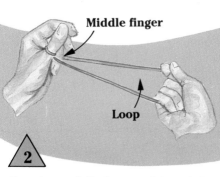

Middle finger
Loop

2 Put the middle finger of your left hand into the loop you have made by twisting the band.

Floating Band

This effect is hard to do fast, but when you can, the band seems to float off your fingers. Ask someone to copy you. It is not as simple as it looks.

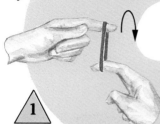

1 Hold an elastic band around your two forefingers and twirl it around them.

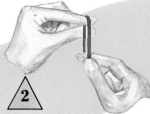

2 Stop twirling and take the band between the forefinger and thumb of both hands.

3 Move your hands together until each thumb touches the opposite forefinger.

4 Now spread your fingers and thumbs and let the band fall onto the table.

Tip

Perform elastic band tricks close to your audience. If they are far from you they cannot see what is going on.

Leaping Band

If you wrap a small band around your first two fingers in a certain way, you can make it jump from one finger to the other. This works even if someone holds the end of your first finger.

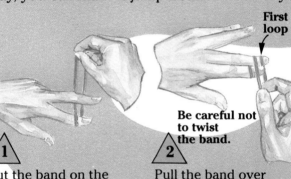

First loop

Be careful not to twist the band.

Volunteer

1 Put the band on the first finger of your left hand. With your right first finger and thumb, pull the band behind your left middle finger, like this.

2 Pull the band over your middle finger to loop onto your first finger again. Ask someone to hold your first finger to stop the band escaping.

3 Now bend your middle finger so that the first loop of the band comes off. The band will jump off your first finger onto your middle finger.

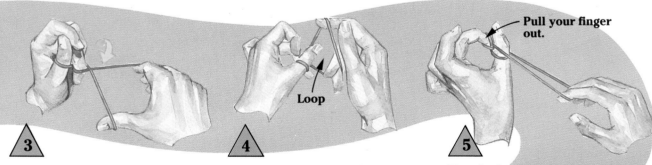

Loop

Pull your finger out.

3 Twist the band again, so that the side further from you comes over the other side of the band.

4 Put the further side of the loop over the top of your left thumb, without taking your middle finger out.

5 Tug the band and pull your middle finger out. The band seems to go straight through your thumb.

Piano Trick

You can do this trick with anything which will fit between someone's fingers, but playing cards are best. It is important to say things correctly so your volunteer comes to the right conclusion. You misdirect * by stressing that a pair is always an even number.

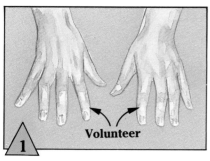

1 Volunteer

Ask a volunteer to put his hands palm-down on the table, with the fingers bent as if he were playing the piano.

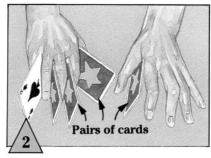

2 Pairs of cards

Start to place pairs of cards between each of his fingers, saying "A pair even" as you put each pair in place.

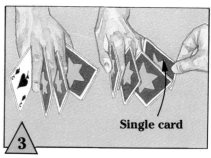

3 Single card

Place a single card between his last two fingers. Make sure the volunteer notices the single card. Say "One card – odd".

4 Magician

Remove the cards in the same order. Take each pair, saying "A pair – even" and divide it, making two piles of cards.

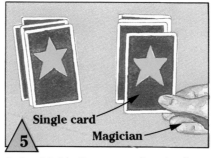

5 Single card — Magician

Ask which pile to put the single card on. Lay it down, saying "An even number plus an odd number is an odd number".

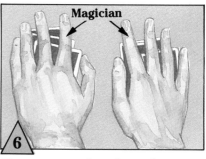

6 Magician

Now put your hands on the two piles of cards, saying you will make the single card move from the odd pile to the even one.

7 Volunteer

Ask the volunteer to count the cards in both piles. The odd pile will have eight cards (even) and the other will have seven (odd).

How it works

As you repeat that each pair is even, the volunteer will not realize that when you divide 7 pairs of cards, you make two piles of 7 (odd) cards. Adding the single card to one pile makes 8, which is even, not odd.

Eleven Fingers

Hold up your fingers in front of you and say you can prove you have 11 fingers. Count the fingers on one hand like this: "10, 9, 8, 7, 6", then look at the other hand and say "And 5 makes 11".

* *See p4 for misdirection.*

Speedy Sum

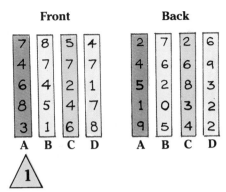

Front   **Back**

7	8	5	4		2	7	2	6
4	7	7	7		4	6	6	9
6	4	2	1		5	2	8	3
8	5	4	7		1	0	3	2
3	1	6	8		9	5	4	2
A	B	C	D		A	B	C	D

1

Cut four strips of paper or cardboard about 15cm (6in) long and 2.5cm (1in) wide. Write the sets of five numbers as shown in the picture on the front and back of the strips.

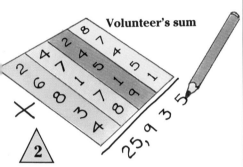

Volunteer's sum

2

Ask a volunteer to mix the strips up and turn them over as much as he likes. Then he should line them up and add together the five four-figure numbers he had made, using a calculator or pen and paper.

$$3715$$
$$22220$$
$$\overline{25,935}$$

Magician's sum

3

While the volunteer is working it out, add the fourth four-figure number to 22220. You will get the same answer as the volunteer, but much faster than him. Amaze him by announcing it straight away.

Counting Sheep

This is a fun story with some silly sums in it. You could illustrate it with sheep made out of paper.

1

A man had a flock of 19 sheep. He wanted to give each of his three children a share: half to the eldest, a quarter to the middle one and a fifth to the youngest.

2

He realized that this plan would involve chopping up sheep. To avoid doing this, he borrowed an extra sheep from one of his friends. Now he had 20 sheep all together.

3

He gave 10 sheep (half) to the eldest, 5 (a quarter) to the middle one, and 4 (a fifth) to the youngest. Then he gave the sheep he had borrowed back to his friend.

How it works

19 is a prime number. It can only be divided by 1 and 19 – not 5, 4, or 2. To avoid chopping up sheep, the man needs a number which can be divided by 5, 4, and 2 – like 20. $1/5$, $1/4$, and $1/2$ only make $19/20$, not 1, so the farmer has one sheep left over to return to his friend.

Vanishing Grape

In this trick, you make a grape vanish and then reappear in your mouth. To do this, you use a sleight of hand called the French Drop. You need to sit at a table to do the trick.

You need two grapes for the trick: one on the table, the other hidden in your right hand. You can hold it Finger Palmed, like this.

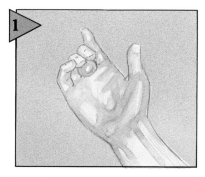

Pick up the grape from the table between the thumb and fingers of your right hand, so that the hidden grape is behind the visible one.

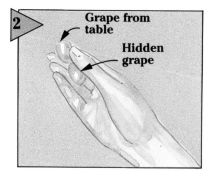

Grape from table

Hidden grape

Put the top grape into your mouth and leave the other one sticking out between your lips. It will look as if you have only one grape in your mouth.

When the audience has seen the grape between your lips, take it out with your right hand. Hold it between your first finger and thumb.

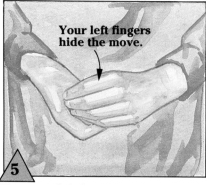

Your left fingers hide the move.

Put your left hand over your right as if to take the grape, but drop it onto your right fingers (a French Drop). Close your left hand as if it has the grape.

Drop you right hand casually into your lap and leave the grape there. At the same time, raise your left hand to the top of your head, watching it move.

Flatten your left hand and hit the top of your head. As you hit your head, spit out the grape from your mouth. Catch it in your right hand.

Tip

Remember not to say anything when you have a grape in your mouth which the audience is not supposed to know about.

Self-Raising Roll

This is a simple trick which is good fun. You need a fork, a bread roll and a napkin.

Practise in front of a mirror until it looks as if the roll is floating up of its own accord.

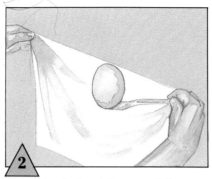

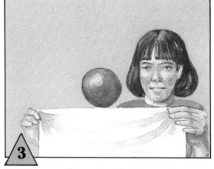

1 Secretly prepare the bread roll by sticking a fork into it at an angle, like this. Leave the roll and fork ready on the table, and lay a napkin over them.

2 Hold the fork with your right thumb and first finger, and a corner of the napkin between your first two fingers. Holding the other corner with your left hand, lift the roll and napkin.

3 Lift the roll on the fork so that it can be seen above the napkin, but don't let the audience see the fork. Move the napkin up and down so that it looks as if the roll is floating.

Coin in Roll

Finding a coin in a bread roll is a good trick to do at the dinner table. Start with a coin Finger Palmed* in your right hand.

Pick up a roll in your left hand and shake it by your ear. **1**

2 Hold the roll in both hands and press your thumbs down into the middle to break it open underneath.

3 Press up into the middle of the roll with your fingers, pushing the coin inside.

View from underneath

4 At the same time, break open the top with your thumbs to show the coin in the middle of the roll.

5 Look at the coin in surprise, pull it out of the roll, and slip it into your pocket.

Tip

Don't draw too much attention to the trick. People will still notice and they might even look for money in their rolls.

* See p59 for how to Finger Palm a coin.

MORE PAPER TRICKS

Paper Fold

This is a simple way of making something small disappear. You need two identical pieces of paper about 9cm (3.5in) square. Follow steps 1-3 to make the prop. Then steps 4-7 tell you how to do the trick.

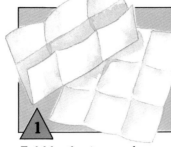

1
Fold both pieces of paper into thirds both ways, so that each piece is divided into nine equal squares.

Glue

2
Fold the paper into two packets with the middle squares as the backs. Stick them back to back.

Folded piece under here

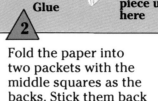

3
Unfold one piece to be ready to do the trick. Keep the other piece tightly folded underneath.

Passport to Heaven

This is more an illustrated story than a trick, but it is entertaining. The speech bubbles tell you what to say and the text below the pictures tells you what to do.

> There were two men trying to get to Heaven, one good and one bad.

1
Take a rectangular piece of paper and fold one of the top corners across to the opposite side of the paper.

> When St. Peter asked for their passports, only the good man had one.

A   B

2
Now fold the other top corner down so that there is a triangle at the top of the sheet, like this.

Crosses Across

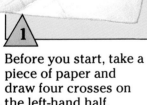

Plain

Crosses

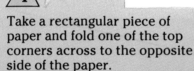

Left   Right

1
Before you start, take a piece of paper and draw four crosses on the left-hand half. Make sure the crosses cannot be seen through the paper.

2
Hold up the paper with the crosses facing you on the left. Tear it down the middle and turn the right-hand half around casually to show it is blank.

3
Put the right-hand piece in front of the left-hand piece, covering the crosses. Turn the pieces over and tear them both in half again.

4
Put the right-hand pieces in front of the left-hand ones and turn them over again. Tear them to make the pieces square. Put the right-hand half in front.

38

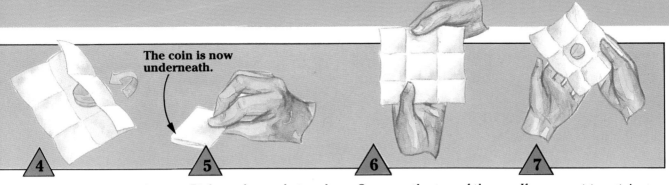

The coin is now underneath.

4
Borrow a coin or a ring from a member of the audience, and fold the top piece of paper around it.

5
Pick up the packet and turn it over causally, so the empty side in on top. Make a magic gesture over it.

6
Open up the top of the packet, keeping the other side hidden. The object you put inside has "vanished".

7
If you want to retrieve the object, fold the packet up. Turn it over again, and unfold it as before.

> The bad man stole the passport and tore it up to stop the good man getting in.

Tear here

B

A

> St. Peter took the pieces from the bad man, and saw he belonged to the devil.

> But the bad man had dropped a piece, which the good man used as his passport.

3
Fold the paper in half so that A is on top of B, and tear two strips down through all the thicknesses.

4
Unfold the smaller pieces and put them together to make a devil shape. Leave the larger piece aside.

5
Pick up the larger piece of paper and unfold it, to show the audience that it is the shape of the cross.

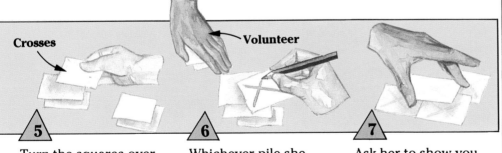

Crosses

Volunteer

5
Turn the squares over and deal them in turn into two piles. The pile you deal to first will contain the crosses. Ask someone to choose a pile.

6
Whichever pile she picks, ask her to cover the one with crosses and give you the other.* Draw crosses on your pieces, then destroy them.

7
Ask her to show you her pieces. They have crosses on them. It looks as if the crosses have moved from your pieces of paper to hers by magic.

Tip

Always practise a trick with its patter, but don't forget when you perform that the story is new to your audience. If you sound bored, you will bore them, too.

Use Magician's Choice to do this - see p5.

39

COINS ON THE MOVE

Disappearing Coin

1 Hold a coin between your left fingers and thumb, and the corner of a handkerchief between the first and second fingers of your right hand.

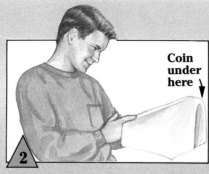

Coin under here

2 Cover the coin with the handkerchief and drag it over the coin, moving your right hand towards you and keeping your left hand still.

3 Do this again, but this time take the coin between your right thumb and first finger as you cover your left hand, still not moving this hand.

Through The Handkerchief

1 Hold a coin between your left forefinger and thumb. Cover the coin with a handkerchief.

2 Take hold of the coin through the handkerchief with your right hand. At the same time pinch a fold of cloth between your left thumb and the coin.

3 Let go of the coin with your right hand and pull up the front of the handkerchief to show the audience the coin is still underneath.

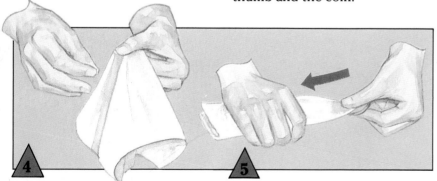

4 As you lower the front of the handkerchief again, flick your left hand so the side of the handkerchief nearest to you goes over to the front as well.

5 With your right hand, slowly pull the handkerchief, leaving the coin in your left hand. It appears to have gone straight through the cloth.

Tip

If your hands are tense and fidgety, try the actors' trick. Shake them hard before you start. It will help you relax.

40

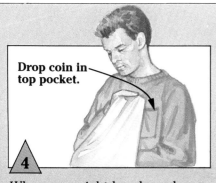

Drop coin in top pocket.

4

When your right hand reaches your shirt front, you can drop the coin in your top pocket. Have something in the pocket to keep it open.

5

Slowly pull the handkerchief right over your hand and show that it is empty. Take the handkerchief in the other hand to show both hands are empty.

Tip

If you are not relaxed when you do a trick, it will make it harder for you to perform it well. Remember: the more you practise, the more relaxed you become.

Reappearing Coin

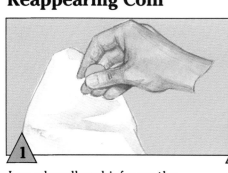

1

Lay a handkerchief over the palm of your left hand and pick up a coin in your right. Move your right hand towards your left, as if to place the coin in the handkerchief.

2

As you go to put the coin in your left hand, curl the fingers of your left hand to hide what you are doing.

3

Press the coin into your right fingers with your thumb, hiding it behind your fingers. Keep it Finger Palmed* as you move your right hand away.

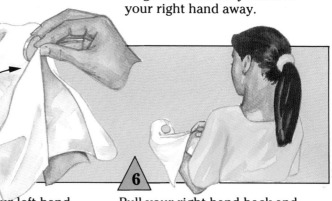

Drop the coin into your left hand.

4

Take the top corner of the handkerchief in your right hand and close your left. Pull the corner down to your left hand and back three times. Open your left hand. It is empty.

5

As you close your left hand, move your right hand forward again with the handkerchief. Drop the coin into your left hand and close your hand.

6

Pull your right hand back and tug at the handkerchief again. Then open your left hand and show the audience that the coin has reappeared.

See p59 for how to Finger Palm a coin.

TRICKS WITH GLASSES

Appearing Glass

This trick has built-in misdirection*. When you pretend to look for a coin in steps 2 and 5, you cover up for taking the glass and moving the handkerchief from one hand to the other.

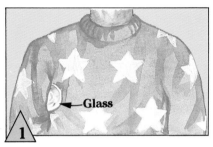

1

To prepare for the trick, secretly put a wine glass in your right armpit, with the base at the front. You could pull a little of your sleeve over the base to hide it.

Glass

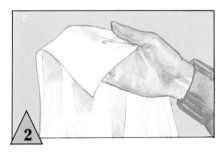

2

Show both sides of a handkerchief. Then drape it over your right hand, holding a corner between your thumb and palm. Hold it so it hides your right armpit.

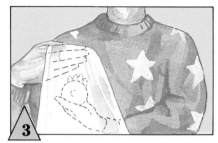

3

Move your left hand behind the handkerchief, saying you are looking for a coin. Now take hold of the glass with the stem between your second and third fingers.

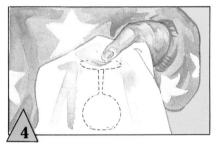

4

Move your left hand forward with the glass and take the handkerchief. Hold the top corner of the handkerchief between your thumb and the base of the glass.

5

Pretend to search your left side for a coin with your right hand. Then take hold of the top of the glass through the handkerchief and stand the glass up on your left palm.

6

Now pull the handkerchief off the top of the glass to reveal it standing on your hand. Polish the glass a little, then shake out the handkerchief and put it in your pocket.

Tip

Don't overact when you are trying to misdirect the audience or they will not be taken in.

Drink Bet

1

Place a full glass on a table. Say you will leave the room and the glass will be empty before you walk in again, although no-one else will touch it. Now walk out.

2

Crawl back into the room, reach onto the table and drink the contents of the glass. Crawl out of the room and then walk in again. You have won your bet.

*** See p4 for misdirection.**

Three Glass Trick

Put three glasses in a row on the table, with the middle one upright and the outside ones upside-down. The trick is to turn them all the right way up in three moves, turning two glasses each time. First demonstrate it to your volunteer like this.

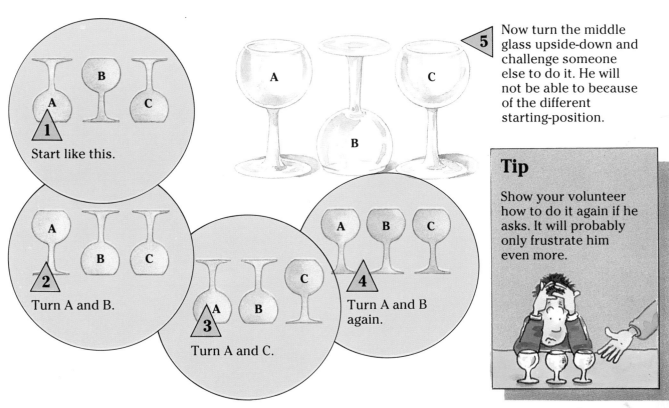

1 Start like this.

2 Turn A and B.

3 Turn A and C.

4 Turn A and B again.

5 Now turn the middle glass upside-down and challenge someone else to do it. He will not be able to because of the different starting-position.

Tip

Show your volunteer how to do it again if he asks. It will probably only frustrate him even more.

Six in a Row

If you have three empty glasses in a row with three full ones beside them, how can you move the glasses so that full and empty glasses alternate? You are allowed three moves, and each time you can only pick up two glasses, which must be next to each other.

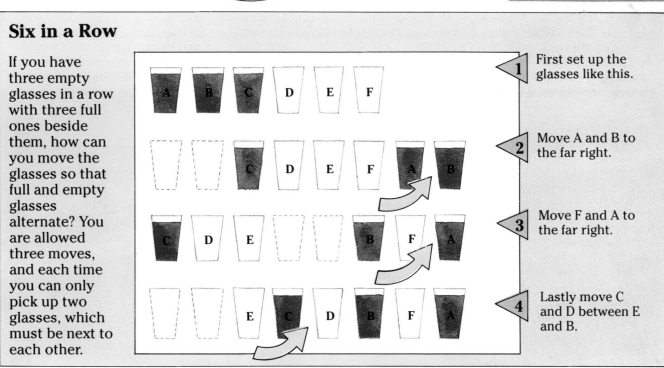

1 First set up the glasses like this.

2 Move A and B to the far right.

3 Move F and A to the far right.

4 Lastly move C and D between E and B.

Salty Knife

This trick uses the Paddle Move: this means that by twisting the knife in your hand, you show the same side twice, but the audience thinks it has seen both sides. Just before you start, secretly wet the blade of a table knife.

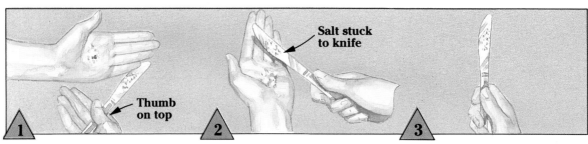

1 In front of the audience, hold the knife with the handle resting on your fingers, and your thumb on top. Pour some salt onto the blade.

Thumb on top

2 Turn the knife over, pretending to pour the salt into your other palm. Close your hand or the audience will see there is no salt in it.

Salt stuck to knife

3 Move the knife so it is upright in your hand with the salty side facing you. The audience must not suspect there is still salt on the knife.

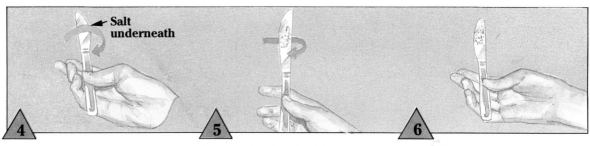

4 Now do the Paddle Move: lower the knife to its position in step 1, twisting it at the same time so the salty side is now facing the table.

Salt underneath

5 Repeat the Paddle Move to raise the knife so that it is vertical, twisting the knife back so the salty side is facing you again.

6 Now pretend to throw the salt in your other hand back at the knife, and lower the knife without twisting it to show the salt on the blade.

Tip

You could do these tricks to brighten up a meal. Everything you need is on the dinner table.

Sticky Fork

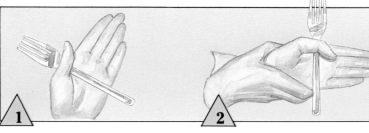

1 Lay your left hand palm-up on the table, and position a fork across your palm, like this. Hold it there with your left thumb.

2 Raise your hand with your palm towards you, holding the fork with your thumb, and your wrist with your right hand.

Spoon Bending

Acting is the key to this trick. If you look surprised at what you have done, the audience will think you have really bent the spoon.

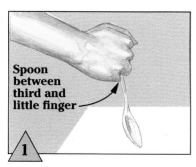

Spoon between third and little finger

1. Hold the handle of a spoon between the third and little fingers of your right hand, with your thumb on top.

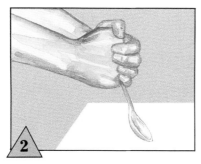

2. Curl your left hand over your right and hold the spoon upright, with the tip of the bowl resting on the table-top.

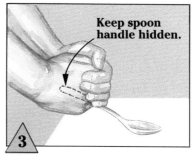

Keep spoon handle hidden.

3. Keeping your hands upright, suddenly bang them down onto the table. It looks as if you have bent the spoon.

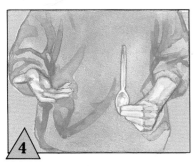

4. Pretend to be embarrassed for a moment. Then show the spoon and let everyone breathe a sigh of relief.

Tip

The only way to convince your audience that you are really bending the spoon is to pretend you are making some effort. If it looks too easy, no-one will be fooled.

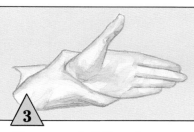

3. Move your left thumb away from your palm and watch the fork drop. Pretend to be disappointed and apologize to your audience.

4. Start again but this time as you raise your hand, extend your right first finger to hold the fork to your palm, unseen by the audience.

5. Slowly move your thumb away, leaving the fork "stuck" to your palm. After a while, drop the fork as if its power has worn off.

THE GLIDE

The Glide is a way of taking the next to bottom card from the pack but looking as if you are taking the bottom card. You may find this sleight difficult, but keep practising.

If you use new, smooth cards you may find it easier. When you can do the Glide without looking at your hands, try the tricks on these two pages.

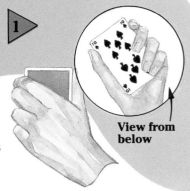

1 Pick up the pack face-down with your thumb on one long side and your fingers on the other. Curl your second and third fingers far enough under the pack to get a grip on the bottom card. This is the Glide position.

View from below

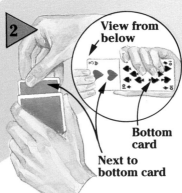

2 Now do the Glide: as you reach to take a card with your other hand, pull the bottom card back with your second and third fingers. Take the next to bottom card. Then slide the bottom card back into place with your fingers.

View from below

Bottom card

Next to bottom card

Red and Black

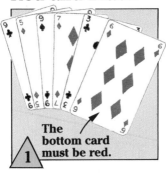

1 The bottom card must be red.

Arrange three red and three black cards of any suit and value in a fan, alternating the colours. Show them to the audience.

2

Holding the six cards in the Glide position, take the bottom card. Show it, saying "red", and put it on top of the others.

3

Now take the new bottom card, saying "black". Show it to the audience and put it on top of the cards, as you did the red one.

4 Glide out black card.

For the third card, Glide out the next to bottom card, saying "red". Put it on top of the cards without showing it.

5 Red card – say "black".

Next take the bottom card again, and without showing it to the audience, say "black", and put it on top of the cards.

6

Take the new bottom card, saying "red", and show it to the audience before putting it on top of the other cards.

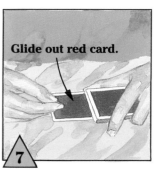

7 Glide out red card.

Lastly, do the Glide again and take the next to bottom card. Say "black", and put it on top of the cards without showing it.

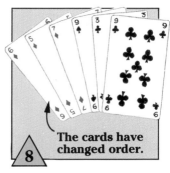

8 The cards have changed order.

Deal the cards face-down, saying "black, red, black, red, black, red". Snap your fingers and turn the cards face-up.

One in Three

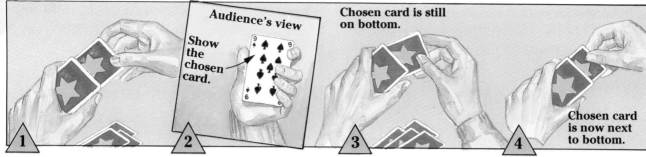

1 Shuffle the pack. Then hold it in the Glide position. Start dealing cards from the bottom of the pack, asking a volunteer to tell you when to stop.

2 Audience's view — Show the chosen card. When he does, show him the card on the bottom of the pack, without looking at it. Turn the pack down again and Glide out the next to bottom card.

3 Chosen card is still on bottom. Tell the volunteer that you will now lose his card in the pack. Slide the card into the middle of the pack without showing it to him.

4 Chosen card is now next to bottom. Now Glide out another card, show it and say, "If you had stopped me one card later this would be your card." Put it on the bottom of the pack.

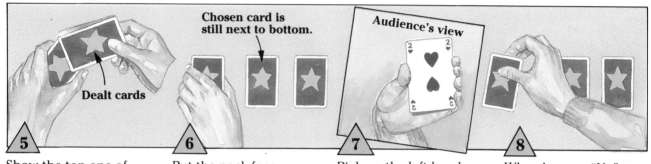

5 Dealt cards — Show the top one of the dealt cards and say "If you had stopped me one card earlier this would be your card." Put the dealt cards on top of the pack.

6 Chosen card is still next to bottom. Put the pack face-down. Say you will cut the pack to find the chosen card. Cut off a third and put it to the right and another third to the left.

7 Audience's view — Pick up the left-hand pile in the Glide position and show the volunteer the card on the bottom, asking whether it is his chosen card.

8 When he says "No", turn the cards down again, then take this card off the bottom and put it face down. Lay this pile of cards to one side.

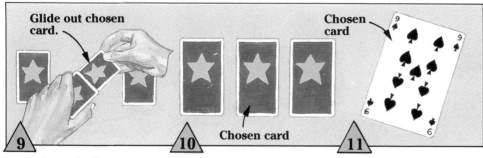

9 Glide out chosen card. Next show the bottom card of the middle pile in the same way, but Glide out the next to bottom card. Put this card to the right of the first one.

10 Chosen card. Repeat steps 7 and 8 with the last pile, putting the bottom card to the right of the other two. Pretend to be disappointed at not finding the card.

11 Chosen card. Ask him to point to one of the cards. Us Magician's Choice* make sure he takes middle card, then a: him to show it. It is chosen card.

Tip

One in Three can be rather a long trick, so make sure your victim is a willing one before you start.

* For Magician's Choice see p5.

MENTALISM

Mentalist tricks are mind-reading effects or tricks where the magician seems to make things happen just by the power of thought.

These tricks are perhaps best performed with quiet confidence, although they can be very light-hearted.

Coincidence

This trick is a mentalist joke, which is good for a comical end to an act or a bit of fun with friends.

1 Ask someone to write any word on a piece of paper, saying you will read his mind and write exactly the same on your piece of paper. Encourage him to choose a word you will not know.

2 Pretend to concentrate hard on him as he writes his word.

3 Now write the words EXACTLY THE SAME on your piece of paper.

4 Ask him to reveal his word.

5 Announce triumphantly that you have accomplished the most difficult feat in mentalism: you have written exactly the same. Show what you have written to prove it.

Hypnotized Fingers

This is an effect which actually happens naturally, but which you appear to cause yourself.

Ask someone to clasp her hands tightly, extending her middle fingers, and hold them apart like this, keeping the others clasped.

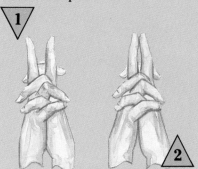

1

2

Move your hand towards hers, making a winding motion as if willing her fingers together. They will slowly move together.

Crazy Clock

1 To make the crazy clockface, cut a large circle of cardboard. Draw lines on one side to divide it into 12 equal sections. Write the numbers 1-12 in a jumbled order in the sections, and punch a hole in each section. Turn it over to prepare the other side.

2 Divide this side into 12 equal sections to match the ones on the other side. Write one letter of THE QUICK DOGS in each section, matching each letter to a number on the other side: T=12, H=11, E=10, Q=9, U=8, I=7, C=6, K=5, D=4, O=3, G=2, S=1.

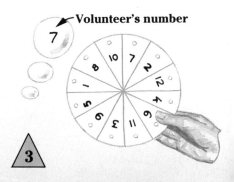

Volunteer's number

7

3 Ask a volunteer to pick a number on the crazy clockface. Say you will reveal his number by tapping the letters on the other side as he counts from 20 back to his number.

Find the Key

For this trick, you need a padlock with two keys which fit it, and three similar keys which do not. You need five identical envelopes and a bag to put them in.

1 To prepare for the trick, seal one of the keys which fit the lock in an envelope. Mark one corner on each side of the envelope with a pencil dot, and put it in the bag.

2 Ask four volunteers to check that only one of the four keys fits the lock. Ask them to mix the keys up and seal each one in an envelope. Put the envelopes in the bag.

Keep the marked envelope apart from the others.

3 Now take an envelope from the bag. Hold it to your head as if you are concentrating on it. You can see if it is marked. If if is not, lay it aside and take another envelope.

4 If you have taken four without finding the marked one, say you will start again. Push aside the envelope left in the bag so you can find it easily. Put the others back in the bag.

5 When you find the marked envelope, tear it open and give the key to the volunteer to try. It will open the lock. Casually tear up the envelope and throw it away.

Volunteer counts silently.

20, 19, 18...

4 Turn the clockface over so only the letters show. Ask him to count silently, one number for each letter you tap. When he reaches his number, he must say "Stop".

12...

5 Tap letters at random for the first eight taps, counting silently. For the ninth, tap the letter T, then tap letters in order, starting to spell out THE QUICK DOGS.

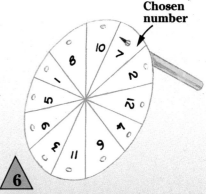

Chosen number

6 When he says "Stop", push the pencil through the hole in the section you are tapping. Show him the other side. The pencil goes through to his chosen number.

Vanishing Pencil

The pencil vanishes up your sleeve in this trick, so wear something long-sleeved. Start with a pencil in your right hand and a handkerchief draped over your left.

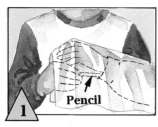

1

Move your right hand towards your left, taking the pencil under the handkerchief. As you do this, secretly push the pencil up your sleeve.

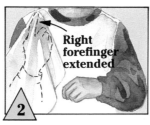

Right forefinger extended

2

Now extend your right forefinger and move your right hand away, covered by the handkerchief. It looks as if you are still holding the pencil.

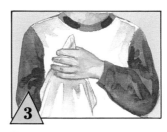

3

Take hold of your finger through the handkerchief with your left forefinger and thumb. Pull a couple of times and then give a sharp tug.

4

Pull the handkerchief off your right hand, bending your finger so you only reveal your empty hand. Shake the handkerchief. The pencil has vanished.

Fly Catcher

Steps 1-4 show you how to make a prop out of a piece of paper, and steps 5-8 suggest a way to use it. This is a trick which you can play on an unsuspecting friend.

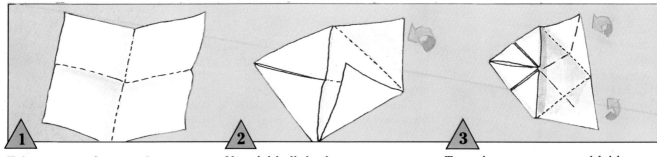

1

Take a piece of paper about 20cm (8in) square. Fold it in half both ways.

2

Next fold all the four corners into the centre.

3

Turn the paper over and fold the four corners into the centre

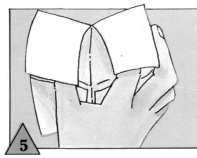

5

Now fit your your first fingers and thumbs into the pockets on the other side of the sheet.

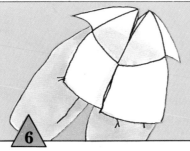

6

Bring your fingers and thumbs together. By moving them differently you can show blank paper or flies.

7

Hold the catcher up to someone's mouth, showing the blank paper, and ask them to breathe into it.

Colour Pencil

Take a pencil out of your pocket, telling your friends it can write any colour they say. If someone says "red", twirl the pencil mysteriously. Then write RED on a piece of paper and give it to them.

Draw some flies in four sections, like this.

4

8

As you take the catcher away, change it to show the flies to your victim, saying "Urggh".

1 Lay a handkerchief flat on the table and place a pencil roughly in the middle of it, like this.

2 Fold the handkerchief diagonally, so that the top corner overlaps the one underneath by about 2.5cm (1in). Put a pencil of a different colour on top of the first one.

3 Roll up the handkerchief around both pencils.

4 Continue until you have rolled over one corner, so that the handkerchief looks like this.

5 Flick over the corner on the roll to cover the one still on the table. Hold it down.

6 Unroll the handkerchief, still holding this corner down. The pencils have swapped places.

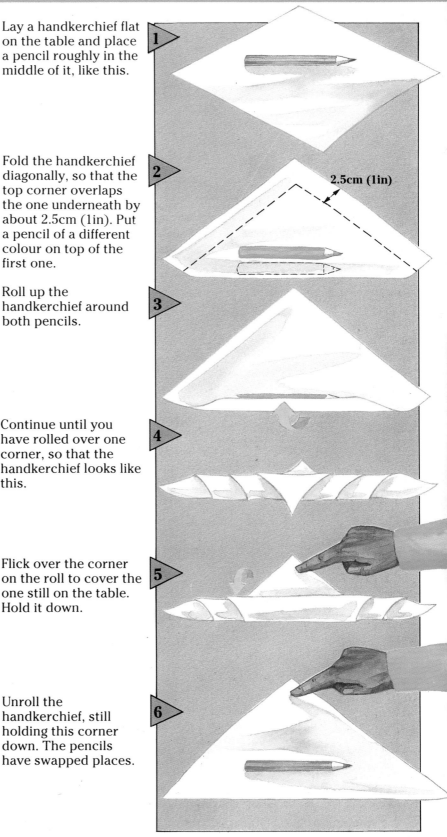

2.5cm (1in)

FIND THE COIN

Coin Through Hand

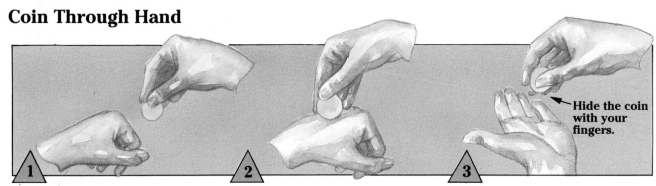

Hide the coin with your fingers.

△1 Hold a coin between the thumb and first three fingers of your right hand. Say you will push the coin through the back of your left hand into your fist.

△2 Push the coin against the back of your hand, and let it slide up between your fingers and thumb. It looks as if the coin is going through your hand.

△3 Turn your left hand over and open it, without moving your right hand. Say disappointedly that the coin must be stuck halfway through.

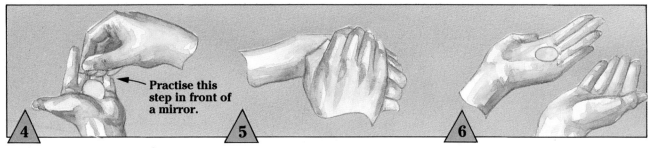

Practise this step in front of a mirror.

△4 As you are closing your hand to try again, drop the coin from your right hand into your left. The fingers of your left hand will hide this move.

△5 Make your left hand into a fist again. Now rub the back of your fist with the fingers of your right hand, as if you are pushing the coin through.

△6 Turn your left hand over, saying you think the coin has arrived. Then open your fist to show that the coin is in the palm of your left hand.

Through the Table

Sit at a table with two coins near each other and close to the edge. Keep your legs together to catch a coin in your lap in step 4. For the trick to work best, keep the rhythm of the moves the same all the way through the trick.

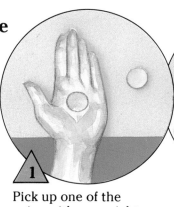

△1 Pick up one of the coins with your right hand and put it in your left palm. Show it to the audience, saying "I need two coins to do this trick. This is the first one".

△2 Turn your left hand over and slap the first coin on the table. At the same time, slide the second coin to the edge of the table with your right hand and pick it up.

△3 Put the second coin in your left palm and show it to the audience, saying "And this is the second". As you slap it down, pick up the first coin again with your right hand.

Vanishing Coin

In this trick, you make a coin vanish into your trouser leg. Start by pressing the coin against the material of your trousers with your right thumb.

Pinch the material at the bottom of the coin with your right first finger. Fold it upwards to cover the coin, turning it over to rest against your thumb.

Hold the top of the fold in place with your left first finger, and take your right hand away, with the coin between your thumb and first three fingers.

Move your right hand, still holding the coin, below your left hand and tug the fold out of the material. The coin has vanished into your trouser leg.

Rubbing It In

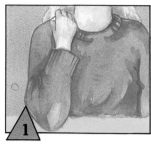

Bend your right arm to rest your hand against your neck, like this. Hold a coin in your left hand and say you will rub it through your sleeve.

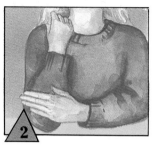

Hold the coin in your left palm and rub it against your right elbow. Take your hand away. Pretend to be disappointed when the coin drops to the floor.

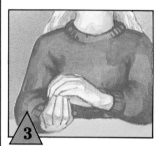

Pick up the coin in your right hand and say you will try again. Pretend to take the coin with your left hand, but French Drop it into your right.*

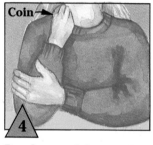

Coin →

Bend your right arm and rub it again. At the same time drop the coin inside your collar. Take your left hand away. The coin has vanished.

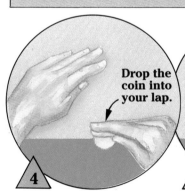

Drop the coin into your lap.

Put the first coin in your left hand and show it, saying "This is the first coin". Slap it down and slide the second coin to the edge of the table and drop it into your lap.

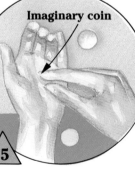

Imaginary coin

Lift your right hand as if it has a coin in it, and put this imaginary coin into your left hand. Close your left hand over it and say "And this is the second coin".

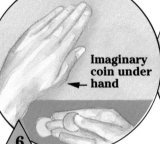

Imaginary coin under hand →

Pick up the first coin with your right hand and take it under the table. Now slap your left hand down and pretend to push the second coin through the table.

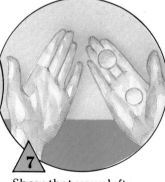

Show that your left hand is empty. At the same time, take the second coin from your lap with your right hand. Bring both coins above the table to show to the audience.

See p36 for the French Drop.

CARD FLOURISHES

A flourish in magic is something designed to catch the audience's attention. These pages explain how to do two flourishes with playing cards, and two tricks which use them. Try the tricks when you can do the flourishes really well.

The Riffle Shuffle

This flourish is an impressive way of shuffling cards which a lot of card players use. It is easier to do on a soft surface, so practise on a chair or carpet at first.

1 Divide the pack into two roughly equal halves. Square them up and place them face-down on the table, side by side.

2 Put your first fingers on top of the cards, with your other fingers on the outside long edges and your thumbs at the top inside corners.

3 Pushing the edges furthest from you down on the table with your fingers, lift the top inside corners of both halves with your thumbs.

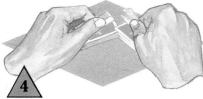

4 Now move the two halves together, so the lifted corners overlap. Lift your thumbs slowly, letting cards drop off the bottom of both halves.

5 Carry on riffling the pack like this until all the cards have fallen, and the corners of the two halves of the pack are completely interlaced.

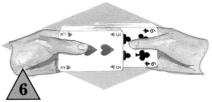

6 Now stand the cards on one long edge, interlacing the ends more. Push the halves into each other with your fingers until the pack is squared.

Riffle Location

Memorize this card.

1 Before you start, you need to set up the pack with all the clubs on top. They can be in any order. Memorize the top card.

Volunteer

2 Ask a volunteer to deal any number of cards between 1 and 12 face-down, and then to memorize the next card in the pack.

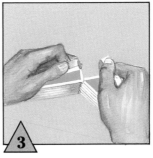

3 Next he should put it back, with the dealt cards on top of it. He should cut the pack and give it to you. Do two Riffle Shuffles.

Magician's card   Volunteer's card

4 Now look through the pack for the card you memorized. The volunteer's chosen card will be the club to the right of it.

The Charlier Cut

This flourish is a one-handed cut which takes some practice, but which looks very good once you have perfected it. Do it quite slowly so the audience can see.

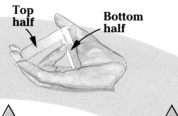

1 Hold the cards by the long edges, face-down over your palm like this. Move your thumb slightly to let the bottom cards fall into your palm.

2 Push the bottom half of the pack up and over the edge of the top half, using your first finger. Your other fingers should stay straight as you do this.

3 As the bottom half comes up level with the top half, let go with your thumb, so that the top half drops into your hand under the bottom half.

4 Move your first finger out from under the pack. Now square up the edges of the pack with your fingers and thumb, and the cut is complete.

Jumping Aces

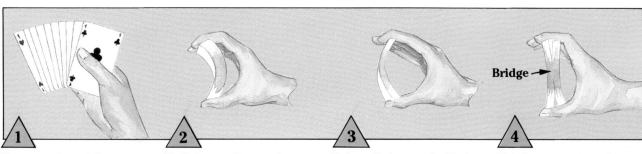

1 To start the trick, openly put the ace of hearts on top of the pack and the ace of clubs at the bottom of the pack.

2 Tell the audience that you are going to do something spectacular, and as you say it, bend the whole pack like this.

3 Take off the top half of the pack and bend it the other way. Do this in a flourishy way to fit the character of the trick.

4 You have now made a "bridge" in the pack. If you hold the cards gently when you cut them, they will cut at this place.

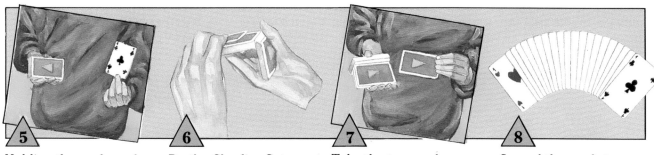

5 Holding the pack ready to do the Charlier Cut, take the ace of clubs from the bottom of the pack. Name it and show it.

6 Do the Charlier Cut up to step 3. Then put the ace of clubs in between the halves of the pack just before you complete the cut.

7 Take the top card. Name it as the ace of hearts without showing it and put it into the pack while cutting, as in step 6.

8 Spread the cards to show the aces have jumped back to their original positions at the top and bottom of the pack.

55

Quick Knot

This way of tying a simple knot works well with string or rope. It works so smoothly that the knot just seems to appear. You need a piece of string about 1m (1 yard) long.

Hold the string in your hands like this, with one end hanging behind your left hand and the other in front of your right palm.

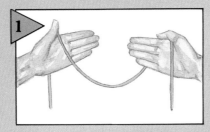

Bring your hands together so your right goes behind your left, parting the first and second fingers of each hand in a scissors action.

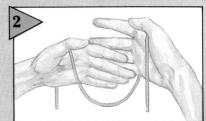

Now take hold of the string behind your left hand with your right fingers, and the string in front of your right hand with your left fingers.

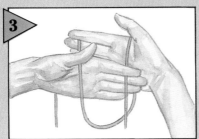

Pull your hands apart again, still holding the string between your fingers. A knot automatically appears in the string as your hands part.

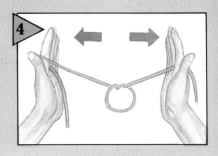

Free the Loop

In this trick, you make a loop escape from a piece of string. Don't say how many knots you are tying in step 3, or someone may check and see there is an extra knot at the end.

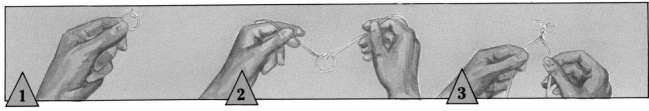

1 Before you start, make a loop by gluing a simple knot into a small piece of string. Put it in your back pocket.

2 Now tie a simple knot into a length of string. Pull it to make a loop the same size as the one in your pocket.

3 Tie the ends of the string together with several knots. Explain that they will keep the loop on the string.

4 Hold the string behind your back, saying you will remove the loop. Put your fingers into the loop.

View from behind

5 Still holding the string behind your back, pull the loop wider until it meets the knots at the ends of the string.

View from behind

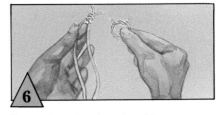

6 Secretly take the glued loop from your back pocket. Show it to the audience, separate from the string.

The Great Escape

This trick works best with two volunteers, as it is fun to watch. You can take part yourself if you have only one volunteer. You need two pieces of string about 1.5m (1.5 yards) long. The volunteers are called A and B to make it easier to follow the instructions.

1 Tie the ends of one piece of string to A's wrists, like this. Tie the knots carefully and make sure they cannot come undone by accident.

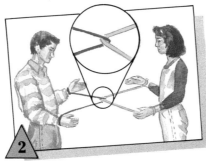

2 Now tie one end of the second string to B's left wrist. Pass it over and back under A's string. Then tie the other end to B's right wrist.

3 Give your friends five minutes to try to get apart without untying the strings. When they give up, tell them how to free themselves.

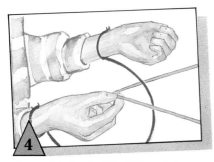

4 A must take hold of the string between B's wrists where it goes over his string, and pull it towards him. B may need to move closer to A.

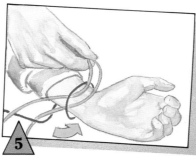

5 A now feeds the loop of B's string up through the string around his own left wrist, towards his hand. He must be careful not to twist it.

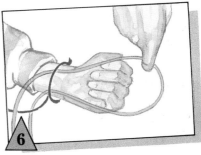

6 A pulls more string up to make the loop larger. Then he closes his left hand to make a fist small enough to pass through the loop.

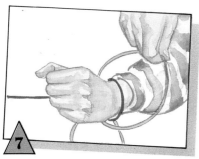

7 Now he passes the loop over his left fist and wriggles the loop over the back of his hand, still without twisting it.

8 A and B can slowly step apart. If they have done everything right, their strings will no longer be joined together.

Tip

You could do The Great Escape as an escapology stunt. Tie the second piece of string to two legs of a table and follow A's moves to escape.

JUMPING COINS

Coin Leap

This is quite a hard trick, although it can be done well with lots of practice. You need four identical coins for this trick.

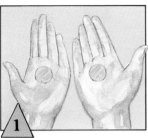

1 Place a coin in each of your palms. Close your hands, saying you will make a coin leap from one hand to the other.

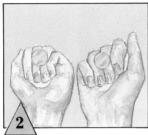

2 Ask a volunteer to put the other coins on your fingers. Shake your hands as if to make the coins jump.

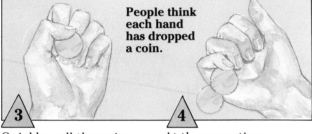

People think each hand has dropped a coin.

3 Quickly pull the coin on your left hand into your palm with your thumb. The shaking should help hide this move from the audience.

4 At the same time, shake the coin off your right hand and open your hand to let the coin in your right palm fall onto the table as well.

Volunteer

5 Apologize for having made a mistake and ask the volunteer to put the coins back on your hands. Then start shaking them as before.

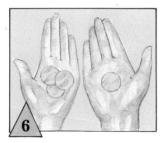

6 While you are shaking them, pull both coins into your palms with your thumbs. Open your hands to show one has "leapt" across to your left hand.

Tear the Coin

In this trick you fold up a coin in a piece of paper. You tear up the paper immediately, and the coin has vanished. You need a fairly large coin and a piece of paper 10cm (4in) square.

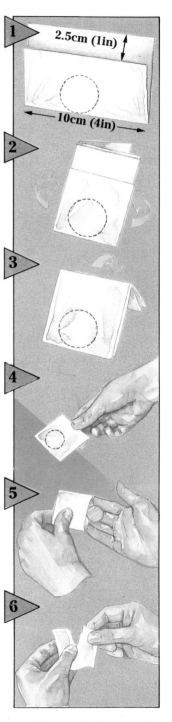

1 Fold the paper so that one side is about 2.5cm (1in) shorter than the other. Drop the coin into the fold.

2.5cm (1in)

10cm (4in)

2 Holding the paper with the shorter side towards you, fold the sides back behind the coin, like this.

3 Now fold the top 2.5cm (1in) behind the coin. You have made a pocket around the coin, with one end left open.

4 Take the pocket by the middle of the open end. Tap it on the table with your right hand to prove that the coin is still inside.

5 Take the pocket by the other end in your left hand, letting the coin slide out into your right hand. Finger Palm it.*

6 To finish, tear the paper into pieces and drop the bits. Put the coin in your pocket when no-one is looking.

* See p59 for how to Finger Palm a coin.

Hand to Hand

In this trick, you appear to transfer a coin twice from your right hand to your left by magic. You need five identical coins, four on the table and one Finger Palmed in your right hand. You need to keep a steady rhythm going when tossing the coins from hand to hand.

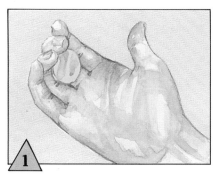

1

To Finger Palm a coin, rest it against the bottom joint of your middle two fingers. Bend them to hold it, leaving your other fingers relaxed.

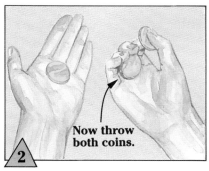

Now throw both coins.

2

Pick up a coin with your right hand and toss it across to your left. Repeat this, and this time throw the Finger Palmed coin as well.

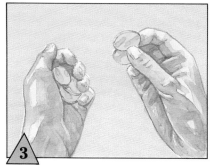

3

Pick up the other two coins with your right hand. Then close both of your hands and pause for a moment to make a grand magic gesture.

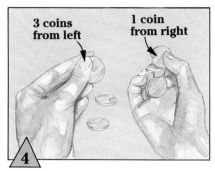

3 coins from left   1 coin from right

4

Drop the coins in your left hand on the table one by one. Also drop one coin from your right hand, keeping the other one Finger Palmed.

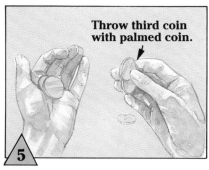

Throw third coin with palmed coin.

5

With your right hand, pick up and throw three coins to your left hand, one by one. Throw the Finger Palmed coin with the third one.

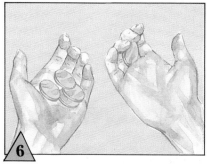

6

Pick up the remaining coin and leave it Finger Palmed in your right hand. Close your hands and make another magic gesture.

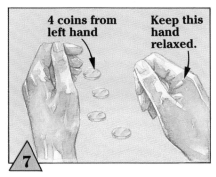

4 coins from left hand   Keep this hand relaxed.

7

Drop the four coins from your left hand one by one. Don't look at your right hand, and try to keep it relaxed, so it appears to be empty.

8

To finish the trick, casually pick up the four coins from the table in your right hand, one by one. Then put all five coins into your pocket.

Tip

When you have something hidden in your hand, don't make it obvious by holding your hand stiffly or by paying too much attention to it.

CARD SLEIGHTS

On these two pages you can learn how to do two sleights: the Backslip and the Palm.

Under the explanation of each sleight is a trick you can do using it.

The Backslip

This is one of the easiest card sleights, although it still takes practice. It is a way of cutting the cards to end up with the top card of the pack on top of the bottom half.

Left side

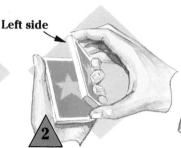

Grip top card.

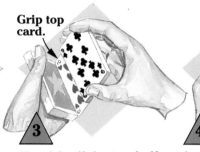

1 Hold the pack face-down in your left palm, with your thumb against one long edge and your fingers curled around the other edge.

2 Take hold of the top half of the pack by the short edges with your right fingers and thumb. Lift the left side of the cards, like opening a book.

3 Now lift off the top half completely, gripping the top card with your fingers to pull it onto the bottom half of the pack. Do this quite quickly.

4 As you slide the top card off the pack, turn your left palm down to hide the move. If you do it all smoothly, no-one should notice the sleight.

Card Switch

Chosen card 6th in pack

Chosen card now 5th

Volunteer

1 Ask someone to think of a number between 5 and 15. Show her the top 15 cards and ask her to memorize the one at her chosen number.

2 Now put the 15 cards back on top of the pack and cut the pack, doing a Backslip so that the top card goes onto the bottom half.

3 Give your volunteer the top half of the pack, keeping the bottom half yourself. Ask her to check quickly and confirm that her card is still there.

Volunteer

Volunteer's card is on your cards.

Volunteer thinks this is her card.

Chosen card

4 Now ask her to tell you the number she chose and count that many cards, less one, back onto your half of the pack.

5 Say you will pick a card by cutting your half of the pack, and do another Backslip at the same time.

6 Ask her to turn her top card over, and turn your top card. You have her chosen card on your half of the pack.

The Palm

Palming a card is hiding it in the palm of your hand. It takes a lot of practice, but will not be noticed when you can keep your hand relaxed with a card in it.

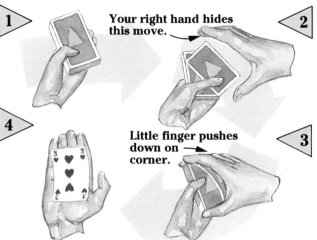

1 ▷ Hold the pack face-down in your left hand with your thumb on top and your fingers against one long side. Hold your thumb slightly bent.

Your right hand hides this move.

◁ **2** Move your right hand to take the pack from your left. At the same time, straighten your left thumb, pushing the top card out at an angle to the others.

4 ▷ The bottom corner of the card should be wedged against the base of your thumb, like this. Hold the pack in your right hand for a moment, then pass it back to your left hand, keeping the card Palmed.

Little finger pushes down on corner.

◁ **3** As you take the pack, push down on the top corner of the angled card with your right little finger and push it up with your left fingers. This levers it into your palm.

Pocket the Card

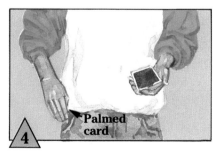

Chosen card

1 Ask someone to think of a number between 1 and 10. Show him the first 10 cards in the pack, counting them as you do so. Ask him to remember the card at his number.

2 Say you will try to find his card and put it in your pocket. Take a card more than ten down, but near the top of the pack. Look at this card, frown and put it on top of the pack.

3 Do this again, but this time, look at the card, smile and put it in your pocket. Now ask the spectator what number he thought of and deal him that number of cards face-down.

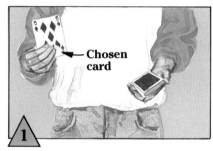

Palmed card

4 Ask the spectator to reveal his top card. At the same time, Palm the top card of the rest of the pack. Ask the spectator whether the card he has turned over is the one he chose.

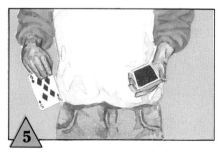

5 When he says "No", reply "Of course not. I have it in my pocket". Reach into your pocket and produce the Palmed card, leaving the other one in your pocket.

Tip

You still have a card in your pocket at the end of this trick. Leave it for a while before taking it out, so people do not connect it with this trick.

MAGIC INFORMATION

Books

There are hundreds of books about magic and magic tricks. Look for them in your local library or a large bookshop. Here are some suggestions of books about specialized areas of magic. You should be able to get them from magic shops, or by mail order.

Introductory books

The Magic Book – Harry Lorayne
The Amateur Magician's Handbook – Henry Hay
Classic Secrets of Magic – Bruce Elliott

History of magic

The Illustrated History of Magic – Milbourne Christopher
The Great Illusionists – Edwin A. Dawes

Presentation and technique

Our Magic – N. Maskelyne and D. Devant
Magic and Showmanship – Henning Nelms
Forging Ahead in Magic – John Booth

Advanced and specialist books

The Royal Road to Card Magic and **Expert Card Technique** – Jean Hugard and Frederick Brauer
The New Modern Coin Magic – J. B. Bobo
It's Easier Than You Think – Geoffrey Buckingham (manipulation)
Anneman's Practical Mental Effects – Ted Anneman
Magic With Faucett Ross – Lewis Ganson (cabaret magic)
The Dai Vernon Book of Magic – Lewis Ganson (close-up and cabaret magic)
The Tarbell Course in Magic (7 volumes) – Harlan Tarbell

Magic conventions

At magic conventions, you can buy tricks, watch magic shows and meet other magicians. They usually last for one or two days. You can find out exact venues, dates and details in magic magazines.

Shops

For magic shops in your area, look in your local telephone directory. These are some well-known ones:

In Britain:

International Magic Studio,
89, Clerkenwell Road,
London EC1R

Tam Shepherds,
33, Queen Street,
Glasgow G1 3EF

In Australia:

Eric's Magic Den,
Myer,
Top of the Mall,
Brisbane

Bernard's Magic Shop,
211, Elizabeth Street,
Melbourne, VIC 3000

In Canada:

Perfect Magic,
4781, Van Horne Avenue
Suite 206, Montreal,
QUE. H3W 1J1

Morrissey Magic Ltd,
2882, Dufferin Street,
Toronto,
ONT. M6B 3S6

In the USA:

Louis Tannen Inc,
6, West 32nd Street,
New York, New York 10001

Abbott's Magic Company,
Colon, Michigan 49040

Mail order

You can get magic books and props by mail order from dealers who advertise in magazines, and from magic retailers.

This company deals in magic by mail order. Please note they only stock specialist books like the ones in the list on the left.

The Supreme Magic Company, Supreme House, Bideford, Devon EX39 2AN, England

Magic courses

Some professional magicians teach magic. If you are interested, although courses may be expensive, try looking in magic magazines for advertisements.

Magazines

You can subscribe to magic magazines or buy them in magic shops. Local clubs may also produce magazines.

In Britain:
Abracadabra,
Goodliffe Publications Ltd,
150, New Road, Bromsgrove,
Worcestershire B60 2LG

In Australia:
Australian Magic Monthly
Contact Tim Ellis (03-481-5832)

In Canada:
There are no Canadian magic magazines. Magic shops should stock British and American magazines.

In the USA:
Genii International Conjuror's Magazine, P.O. Box 3608, Los Angeles CA 90036

Magic societies

There are many magic clubs and societies: local, national and international. Inquire at magic shops to find ones in your area.

Unfortunately, many clubs have restrictions, such as that you must be over 18 or male to join. Two famous international societies are:

The Magic Circle

The Magic Circle is a club which only allows men over 18 to join, but anyone can seek information from them. If you would like to know more about it, write to this address:

The Honorary Secretary,
The Magic Circle,
c/o The Victory Services Club,
63/79 Seymour Street,
London W2 2HF, England

The International Brotherhood of Magicians

This is an international society with groups or "rings" in each country. It has its own magazine, "The Linking Ring".

In Britain:

IBM Secretary, King's Garn, Fritham Court, Fritham, Nr. Lyndhurst, Hampshire SP43 7HH

In Canada:

There are branches of the IBM in many big cities in Canada. Find them in your telephone directory.

In Australia:

Sydney Branch,
Kent Blackmore,
8/33 Muriel Street,
Hornsby, NSW 2077

ACT Branch,
Peter McMahon,
12, Clarkson Street,
Pearce, ACT 2607

In the USA:

IBM Executive Secretary,
P.O. Box 89,
Bluffton,
Ohio 45817

INDEX

First published in 1991 by Usborne Publishing Ltd, Usborne House, 83-85 Saffron Hill, London EC1N 8RT, ENGLAND.
Copyright © 1991 Usborne Publishing.
All rights reserved, No part of this publication may be reproduced, stored in a retrieval system, or transmitted in any form or by any means, electronic, mechanical, photocopying, recording or otherwise, without the prior permission of the publisher.
The name Usborne and the device 🎈 are Trade marks of Usborne Publishing Ltd.   UE   Printed in Belgium.